ROCK YOUR READ-ALOUDS

BY MIKE ARTELL

MAUPIN HOUSE BY
CAPSTONE PROFESSIONAL
a capstone imprint

Page 16 text © Copyright 2017. Brod Bagert

Cover Design: Mike Artell and Rich Parker
Book Design: Rich Parker and Clare Webber

Cataloging-in-publication information is on file with the Library of Congress.
978-1-4966-0845-1 (pbk.)
978-1-4966-0847-5 (E-Book pdf)
978-1-4966-0846-8 (E-Book)

Image credits: all art, Mike Artell
Cover design elements: Shutterstock: Leksus Tuss, oasis15, Olga_C

Capstone Professional publishes professional resources for K–12 educators. Contact us for tailored, in-school training or to schedule an author for a workshop or conference. Visit www.capstonepd.com for free lesson plan downloads.

This book includes websites that were operational at the time this book went to press.

Maupin House Publishing, Inc. by Capstone Professional
1710 Roe Crest Drive
North Mankato, MN 56003
www.capstonepd.com
888-262-6135
info@capstonepd.com

DEDICATION

This book is dedicated to those who give books life by giving them voice.

ACKNOWLEDGMENTS

My deepest thanks to the world-class authors and storytellers who have generously shared their read-aloud tips in this book. I've known some of you many years; others are new friends. I am indebted to you all.

Carmen Deedy
Pam Schiller
Alina Celeste
Mary Jo Huff
Brod Bagert
Mike Shoulders
Frank Levy

CONTENTS

FOREWORD

In 1982 Jim Trelease published the first edition of *The Read-Aloud Handbook*, and since then the daily read-aloud has become a staple in most elementary classrooms and many homes around the country. In his book, now in its seventh edition, Jim provides a rationale for reading to children daily and suggestions for making the read-aloud an integral and special part of school curriculum.

The research behind reading aloud to children is quite impressive (Rasinski, 2010). Dolores Durkin's seminal research in the 1950s found that most children who learn to read before starting school were read aloud to by their parents on a regular (daily) basis. Other research has found that children who are read to on a regular basis are better at comprehending texts and have larger vocabularies than children who are not read to. Moreover, when we read to children in an expressive manner, we provide them with a model of fluent oral reading. And, of course, since most children love to be read to, reading aloud has the potential to lead to higher levels of motivation for and interest in reading, a major concern as children move from grade to grade.

Given how simple it seems at first glance, we may think that we know all there is to know about the read-aloud and how it should be done. Yet, in his new book, *Rock Your Read-alouds*, Mike Artell takes reading aloud to the next level. When reading aloud is done well, it seems to be the easiest thing in the world—choose a book to read to children, sit down in front of them, and read. However, the truth of the matter is that a lot goes into making a read-aloud a special and valued place in the school literacy curriculum for children and for teachers. In his book, Mike takes on these issues so you can create the best read-aloud experience possible. For example, there is much to consider in preparing for the read-aloud. In 15 brief and highly readable chapters, Mike discusses choosing the right book or other material for a read-aloud, but he also asks you to consider things such as how you will introduce the book to children who may not be familiar with the content, genre, or author; how much time to allot to your read-aloud; how you will handle discussion at the end of the read-aloud; how the read-aloud connects to writing; how to create the right environment for the read-aloud; and much, much more.

I am particularly impressed by what Mike has to say about the environment for a read-aloud. Things such as seating, lighting, and even background music can add immensely to the read-aloud experience. Additionally, accoutrements such as props, puppets, pace, and pausing are other factors that you need to consider and for which Mike provides sage advice.

One area I am particularly interested in is reading fluency. Reading aloud provides you with a wonderful opportunity to demonstrate to children what fluent reading sounds like. Of course, in order for your reading to be expressive and fluent, you will need to rehearse your reading. Mike makes it a point to talk about the importance of rehearsal. Your rehearsal itself can become a model for children's own development of reading fluency—for your students to become fluent, they need to rehearse what they read.

If you are looking for a book that will provide you with all you need to make read-aloud the kind of experience that will turn your students on to reading, then *Rock Your Read-alouds* is the book for you. My wish is that every teacher in the country gets his or her hands on this book. If you don't do read-alouds, I think this book will convince you to do so; and if you already do read-alouds, this book will help you make it the memorable experience that you want it to be for children and for yourself.

Timothy Rasinski, PhD
Kent State University

INTRODUCTION

"Everything always becomes a little bit different the moment one speaks it aloud."
Hermann Hesse

Every read-aloud is a performance and a performance will vary depending on the subject matter. I remember reading Edgar Allan Poe to my daughters outside on our patio under a jet-black sky, with barely enough light to see the words. Those read-alouds were not noisy circus acts. The nature of the stories dictated a solemn, sinister mood. I also recall times when we were riding in the car together and I would entertain the kids with an over-the-top recitation of "The Jabberwocky." It's not necessary to be a stand-up comic every time you read aloud; what is necessary is that you tailor your performance to the material, the audience, and your goal for the reading.

I've organized this book around the main elements of a read-aloud. These include choosing an appropriate read-aloud book, creating an appealing environment in which the read-aloud will take place, using pacing and vocal dynamics during the read-aloud, and planning the read-aloud experience to allow for interaction and follow-up.

This book will help you get started if you're new to read-alouds, and it will help you refresh your skills if you've been reading aloud for many years. But it will be up to you to bring your own personality, enthusiasm, and creativity to the read-alouds you do.

The purpose of this book is not to tell you how to read aloud. You already know how to do that. I wrote this book to help you make your read-alouds better. I'll share with you the skills and techniques the very best read-aloud pros use to capture the attention of an audience, hold that audience spellbound, and leave the audience with a powerful memory of the experience. Because the research shows a teacher's read-aloud style can have a terrific impact on a child's appreciation of the written and spoken word, if you apply the techniques in this book when you read out loud to a group of children, I can guarantee that your read-alouds will be more effective, entertaining, and engaging.

When reading aloud is done well, it includes elements of performance and showmanship. Classroom management requires teachers to engage the entire group, and when it's time for the teacher to read aloud, everyone is usually expected to participate. Since we all (especially kids!) have different tastes in reading material, teachers are challenged to make their read-alouds appealing to the largest possible percentage of the class members. A teacher with a rich set of read-aloud performance skills has a better chance of attracting and holding the attention of reluctant readers, or in this case, listeners.

I've watched and heard some magnificent storytellers and gifted read-aloud experts work their magic with children and adults, but one particular episode stands out in my mind.

Shortly after my first picture books were published, I visited a Houston-area school to meet with children in first through fifth grade. Between my second and third presentations, the school's resource teacher asked if I'd like to pop in to see two kindergarten classes. She said I would not have to do a presentation. She just wanted to read one of my books to them. Upon entering the first kindergarten classroom, she asked me to stand in the back of the room and watch. She stood before the class, held up one of my books, and asked the students if they would like her to read it to them. The children were interested, so she sat down and began to read my book out loud. She used a few of the typical read-aloud techniques, such as unusual voices and pointing to the different characters as the text referred to them, but she kept the reading fairly straightforward.

When she finished, she asked students the kinds of questions you might expect. (Did you like that book? What part did you like best?) Then we thanked the students and their teacher and left the room. It had been a pleasant experience albeit rather low-key.

As we walked down the hall, the resource teacher said, "Now watch this." We turned into another classroom and again greeted the children and teacher. Once again, I stepped to the back of the room so as not to distract from the attention the resource teacher needed.

When she began her read-aloud this time, her approach was vastly different. She held up the same book and looked at it as if it was something precious and wonderful. Then she turned to the children and smiled. "Children, this is one of the funniest books I've read in a long time. It has silly animals with crazy names. Look . . . " She held up the book and turned a few pages. The children responded with laughter. "And these animals are pets! Do you have a pet?" There was a great deal of excited feedback from the kids about their pets. "Would you like a pet like this (showing an illustration from the book)?" "YES!" everyone replied. There was more laughter. "Would you like me to read this book to you?" "YES!" again.

Then she read the book with so much energy and attention the children couldn't help but be enthralled by what she was saying. Her voice changed, her pace quickened and then slowed, she gestured, she varied the speed at which she turned pages—sometimes using page turns as a cue that the students were expected to predict the last word to the rhyming verse. When she turned the last page and closed the book, I heard the children say, without any prompting, the words every children's book author lives to hear: READ IT AGAIN!

It was the same book and the same teacher. And the students were basically the same. What changed was the presentation, the delivery—her performance. And that performance changed how the two groups of children experienced the story.

If you choose to apply some of the techniques in this book to your read-alouds, I hope you'll share your experiences with me. I'd love to hear what worked and what didn't work for you. Thanks for all you do to enrich the lives of children.

Mike Artell

mike@mikeartell.com

STORY READING VERSUS STORYTELLING

It is important to realize a book is more than ink on paper or pixels on a screen. A book is a conversation between a writer and a reader. Reading aloud expands that conversation to include the audience member who is hearing and seeing the book being read by the reader. When each audience member feels as though he or she is part of the conversation, the book becomes more than words and pictures; it becomes part of that child's growth and education. The word "educate" comes from the Latin word "educere," which means "to draw out." When reading aloud is done well, the audience is drawn out of themselves and into the story.

> *"In books I have traveled, not only to other worlds, but into my own."*
> Anna Quindlen

I want to acknowledge the difference between reading aloud (also known as story reading) and storytelling. Storytelling is not limited by the actual text in a book and that gives the storyteller more flexibility in the performance. Two story readers reading the same version of *Goldilocks and the Three Bears* from a book might vary the performance elements of their read-aloud, but the words they were reading out loud would be essentially the same. Two storytellers, on the other hand, would almost certainly not use precisely the same words to tell the same story. A good example of how story readers are wedded to the text can be found in the wonderful book, *The Book with No Pictures* by B.J. Novak.

The book tells the listener that the reader must read the words EXACTLY as they are written. This seems normal enough until the reader begins to read a series of nonsense words and ridiculous sounds. If the reader is clever, he or she will express increasing dismay that he or she is trapped and can only get out of this predicament by stumbling through the text while sounding completely foolish—much to the delight of the young listeners.

Novak defuses potential reading reluctance by acknowledging up front that the book looks boring and serious. But then he brilliantly explains the one important difference between story reading and storytelling by explaining (from the words in the book) that the reader has to read the words exactly as they are written. As he reads aloud, the reader demonstrates that reading the words exactly as they are written can be hilarious.

Despite the title, Novak's book is FILLED with pictures. True, there are no drawings, but the typography itself becomes the imagery. The words are built of a wild variety of fonts splashed with bright, childlike colors. They tumble and collide in a crazy mélange of mixed-case lettering. This is story reading material at its most fun and is a wonderful resource for any adult who doesn't mind being part of the joke.

Novak demonstrates that in story reading, the reader guides the listeners through the story and provides a model for the way a book is to be read. The reader becomes an intermediary between the writer (and illustrator) and the listeners. Although the reader is an important player in the read-aloud, he or she takes no ownership of the story as would the author.

In storytelling, the storyteller does take ownership of the story by the improvisation and variety he or she brings to each telling. In story reading, the focus is on the book; in storytelling, the focus is on the storyteller. This doesn't mean the story is of secondary importance. The focus in storytelling must be on the storyteller because there is no book for the listeners to look at as the story progresses.

In the classroom, story reading works best when the educator wants students to pay attention to the story as it was written by the author and illuminated with images by the illustrator. Storytelling works best when the goal is to have students zeroed in on the educator's words and actions. Story reading focuses on the book. Storytelling focuses on the person.

Storyteller

Story reader

NONTRADITIONAL READ-ALOUD AUDIENCES

If you're reading this book, I assume you do your read-alouds for children in elementary or middle-school grades. However, there is wonderful work being done by people who read aloud to other age groups.

One overlooked audience for read-alouds is high school students. My wife taught high school science and, at the beginning of each school year, she read Dr. Seuss's *The Lorax* to her students. It was great fun for her to see the big, tall football players sitting quietly, listening to a book written for small children. But the truth is, almost everyone likes to be read to. If a high school student is seemingly forced to listen while a teacher reads a book to him or her, well, then that student can enjoy the story without running the risk of looking uncool.

Many older people can no longer see well enough to read a book or they may not have the strength or stability in their hands to hold a book. Church groups and civic organizations often have volunteers who will read to those seniors who can no longer read by themselves.

I spoke at a Summer Institute in Dallas many years ago, and one of the highlights of the event was a late evening session with Carol Hurst. Carol was one of the greatest storytellers I've ever heard, and I had the good fortune to call my friend. The attendees at Carol's session were provided milk and cookies and encouraged to wear their pajamas. After everyone had settled in with a bedtime snack, Carol began to work her storytelling magic. It was surreal to watch a couple hundred grown adults hang on Carol's every word. The room had a stage and wonderful lighting, which lent drama to Carol's storytelling. She commanded attention as she spoke with authority and confidence. But hidden behind that no-nonsense personality was an impish sense of humor. She loved to read and tell stories. It didn't matter if she was talking to small children or adults. Carol knew how to draw her listeners into a story and guide them along the way.

As you hone YOUR skills, consider how you might apply them to other nontraditional audiences.

CHAPTER 2

READ-ALOUDS AS A FUNDAMENTAL BUILDING BLOCK FOR WRITTEN LANGUAGE

"Books shouldn't be daunting, they should be funny, exciting, and wonderful; and learning to be a reader gives a terrific advantage."
Roald Dahl

For decades, former attorney and internationally known poet Brod Bagert has toured the world sharing his love of poetry. In his books and live performances, Brod speaks to children (and adults) in a way that enables them to hear their own voices, engage their own thoughts, and discover their own feelings. Brod believes oral performance of exemplary written text is a vital element in helping children learn to write.

Here's what Brod has to say about the fundamental importance of oral language to other forms of communication:

"We experience language in four ways: We speak, we listen, we write, we read. Each experience strengthens and empowers the other. I think of it as a kind of internal weather system with the potential to build itself into a whirlwind of communicative power. Yet I believe that oral recitation remains the driving force because oral recitation engages our entire self. It is at once physical, emotional, immediate, and intensely personal; a complete mind-body-social-emotional experience.

Consider the act of recitation. We use our abdominal muscles to support breath. We engage the 43 muscles of our face to both project words and to form the facial expressions that communicate emotion. Our ears hear the words we say. Our eyes watch our listeners as they respond. It is an immediate response that converts the aloneness of individual existence into a community of being. It is the imperative that drove our ancestors to invent language. It is the living pulse of language that stimulates hunger for vocabulary and grammar and sentence structure. It is simultaneously both motivational and instructive. It is why writers write. I can only imagine the futility of attempting to teach children without it.

So I offer this simple suggestion. If we want students to write pristine expository-prose, we should give them examples of pristine expository-prose to read aloud. If we want them to write engaging, dramatic monologues, we should give them examples of engaging, dramatic monologues to read aloud. As they recite, they will begin to collect bits and pieces of the good stuff (successful phrasing, effective literary gestures, etc.). They soon begin to recognize similar good stuff in their general reading and bring some of it to their own writing, both of which inspire further dramatic recitation and more reading and more writing. It's a real thing, it happens, and once the process is underway, we as teachers need no longer drag students kicking and screaming into full literacy. Instead, we simply nurture the cycle by continuing to provide exemplary text and the opportunity to perform it."

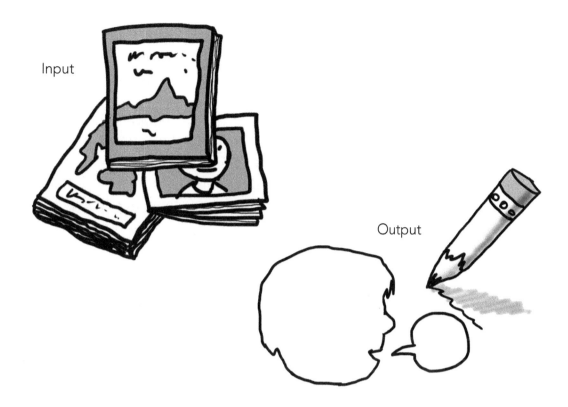

Input

Output

INPUT AND OUTPUT

Reading is a form of communicative input. It is an activity for which the reader internalizes information. Speaking and writing are forms of communicative output. These activities are shared with the world. As I read Brod's words, I am reminded of how much more complicated writing is than speaking. Most two- and three-year-olds can speak enough words to communicate at a basic level. But it would be rare for any of them to write a complete sentence with a subject and a verb. By learning to speak well, we learn (at the appropriate time) to write well. And the point Brod makes is that we learn to speak well by first hearing well-chosen words spoken correctly in the right context.

You know this is true from your own experience. You have met or taught children who come from homes with a rich language environment, and you've seen how they naturally apply many of the most important language skills at an early age. But while it is vital to expose a child to a rich verbal environment, it isn't enough. This is because in every home and classroom, we unconsciously develop a "working vocabulary," which is efficient and makes communication easier. Using that vocabulary increases our chances of understanding family members or teachers and being understood by them. (Note: To my frustration, I've learned this working vocabulary also works with dogs but not cats.) From time to time, a teacher or someone in the family may introduce a new word, but often those words are added because they're essential to the completion of some task. An example might be in the classroom where a child may not be familiar with the word "cubby" as a place to put his or her jacket. Or the word "cafeteria" as a place to eat a meal. While those words do indeed expand the pool of words from which a child picks to communicate, when it comes to building a rich vocabulary, children are more likely to hear words they find new or uncommon by reading them (or hearing them read) from a book. That's because an author may be writing from a perspective a child finds novel (pun intended) and that perspective and experience set may require the use of words with which a child is unfamiliar. This is especially true in the case of children whose home lives are not supportive of a rich, constantly expanding vocabulary.

It is important for a child's language and cognitive development to supplement his or her everyday vocabulary by reading (and hearing read) unfamiliar words on a regular basis. Written text (most often in books) provides the most flexible and effective way of doing that.

There's an old expression that says if the only tool you have is a hammer, every problem begins to look like a nail. To avail ourselves of options, we must first be aware that options exist. Read-alouds introduce young learners to some of their language options.

When I visit schools, I usually spend time showing young children how to draw emotions. We'll draw faces that are happy, sad, frightened, and angry. Whenever I draw the angry faces with children, they almost always identify the faces as "mad." When I ask them to give me another word for "mad," they immediately say "angry." They know the word and its meaning, but it doesn't occur to most of them to choose the more accurate word. That's because children hear the word "mad" used far more often. By giving them an opportunity to use the word "angry" in our drawing exercise, they develop a comfort and familiarity with it and are therefore likely to use it more readily in place of "mad." Read-alouds provide a similar opportunity for children to become comfortable with words they know but rarely use. It then becomes more likely that they will use those "preferred" words in their speech and eventually in their writing.

It's fair to ask why you should read aloud to children when there are other options such as educational TV and videos, as well as digital books that read stories aloud by themselves. I decided to do a quick Google search on the phrase "benefits of reading aloud to children," and I came up with more than one million hits. That's a lot of information and if you need a million or so reasons to read to children, you can find them online. But let me offer one simple reason I believe subsumes all the others: You should read aloud to children because it requires you to invest in them your most precious, non-renewable resource: your time. Children know that. And if they're too young to know it, they can feel it. That's all the reason you need.

ROCK YOUR PREPARATION

> *"I believe that people make their own luck by great preparation and good strategy."*
> Jack Canfield, co-author of the *Chicken Soup for the Soul* series

If you're a talented improvisational comedian or actor, you can stand before an audience with no preparation and deliver a memorable performance. But if you're not an improv pro, don't try to wing it.

"Normally I advise our faculty
NOT to wing it, but in your case..."

THINGS TO CONSIDER AS YOU PLAN YOUR READ-ALOUD:

Have you chosen a book that lends itself to being read aloud?

Are you familiar with the book you've chosen?

Will you use any props or sound effects?

If you do decide to use props or sound effects, decide in advance exactly when you want to introduce them and the logistics of physically handling them. You don't want to have to stop reading and walk to another part of the room to retrieve your prop. Have it nearby and ready to go. See Chapter 6 starting on page 35 for more information about preparing your environment for a read-aloud.

If you use whistles or other sound effects be sure to test them in advance to ensure that they'll produce the sound you want.

Have you scheduled enough time to introduce the book to the children before you read it?

You want to avoid "cold starts" if possible. Plan to have a minute or so to introduce the book to the children. Show them the cover and call attention to the title, the author and illustrator, and any characters or cover imagery that will be important in the story.

Have you scheduled enough time to read the book aloud more than once?

If children like the book, they will likely ask you to read it again. This can be a wonderful way to reinforce elements of the story that you may have had to gloss over during the first reading. If your schedule permits, plan on reading the story twice.

Have you scheduled enough time for interaction with the children as you read the book?

For children to connect with a story, they need to have a chance to ask questions and express their thoughts about what is being read to them. This takes time. It may not be possible to answer every question or give every student an opportunity to comment on the story, but interaction should be part of every read-aloud.

Sometimes this may mean that you may not be able to finish the story in one sitting. That's OK. It's better to come back to a story than to hurry through it.

Have you built in enough time after you read for follow-up questions and discussion?

The interaction following a story is an opportunity to summarize and reflect on what's been read. It's also a time for any follow-up questions children may have. Students who have been puzzled during the reading of the story and who were reluctant to interrupt the flow of the read-aloud with questions can be encouraged to ask questions and make comments following the reading.

Have you mentally rehearsed your read-aloud so you're prepared for the unexpected?

Mentally rehearsing the read-aloud is different from simply reading the book in advance. Like an athlete or a musician that visualizes a performance before the actual event, mentally rehearsing the read-aloud gives you an opportunity to anticipate what is likely to happen during the reading. Imagining the seating, the environment, possible interruptions, and the dozens of other distractions in a typical school day can help you resolve any small issues before they become big issues.

Sometimes the demands of the day will allow for only minimal advanced planning for your read-aloud. Other days you might be able to squeeze in a read-aloud but with only limited interaction with the children. You may choose to read a book with few performance elements because you want to make an overall point about the kind of story you're reading. The classic folktale, *Little Red Riding Hood*, offers a good example. You may wish to read the classic version, then read *Lon Po Po: A Red-Riding Hood Story from China* and then read *Petite Rouge*, my Cajun version of the story. After you have read the three versions, you could display all three books for the children and begin to compare and contrast them. In this situation, you may want to use the books as a trilogy rather than focusing on a full-blown performance for each version. Your focus in this multi-book situation would be broader and not as deep.

LET'S BE REAL

There's a slight chance if you don't read the book in advance and your audience is very forgiving, you may deliver a great performance with little preparation. But if you're not familiar with the story or if you haven't built in enough time to allow for the children's interaction, you're likely to miss opportunities to make a point or provide insight that would have made the reading more meaningful. If you don't know what's coming in the story, you won't know how to give hints to your listeners about something that's about to happen. It will certainly be more difficult to make connections to other stories, life experiences, and curriculum areas. So, at the very least, read the book aloud to yourself first. Being familiar with the book before you read it to a group of children is essential.

CHAPTER

4

HOW TO PICK A
READ-ALOUD BOOK

> *"It is well to read everything of something,*
> *and something of everything."*
>
> Lord Henry P. Brougham

This may be a good time to ask: Why did you select the book you plan to read aloud? Is it a new book everyone is reading and talking about? Is it a classic you loved as a child? Is it one of your state book award nominees? Is it a book that addresses a curriculum need?

RECOGNIZE YOUR READING BIASES

When it comes to reading, we are all biased. And that's not necessarily a bad thing. Here's a question I always ask when I speak to groups about literacy: What book is sitting on your bedside table? If you're like most people I ask, you have a book of fiction on your bedside table. I find that people who are avid readers are almost always readers of fiction. That's not to say they never read nonfiction; only that they prefer fiction.

I once had a discussion with a school librarian about whether or not boys are strictly readers of fiction or nonfiction. I asked the librarian if he was left-handed or right-handed. He said he was right-handed. I asked him if he ONLY used his right hand or if he sometimes used his left hand as well. He smiled at the question and its obvious answer. I explained further that just as we use both hands regardless of our natural handedness, most people read both fiction and nonfiction with a preference for one or the other. When you're choosing a book for a read-aloud, I think it's fair to ask yourself if your own biases are influencing the books you choose to read to students.

"Would you like me to read this book about a sweet little sunflower who loves the earth or THAT book about noisy, smelly race cars?"

READ THE WAY YOU EAT

My belief is everyone, children and adults alike, should read the way they eat. Or more accurately, they should read the way they SHOULD eat. When I say this during my school presentations, the kids always look confused. I explain it this way: Broccoli is good for you. It's full of vitamins and minerals, phytochemicals, and fiber. But if you tried to exist on a diet of nothing but broccoli, you would not be healthy. You wouldn't be getting the broad range of nutrients humans need for good health. Conversely, if you ate nothing but milk chocolate, you would eventually do serious damage to your body as the result of all the sugars and fats in the chocolate. I should probably conduct a test to confirm that statement!

Just as you need to eat a variety of food to be healthy, you also need to read a variety of material to be a good reader. And by "good reader," I don't merely mean someone who understands the words and can pass a comprehension test based on the book. I don't even mean "fluency." By "good reader" I mean someone who brings something TO the book as well as takes something FROM the book. A good reader engages in that conversation with the writer by internalizing the writer's words. By using the writer's words as a link to the reader's own experiences and imagination, the reader connects with the writer.

When it comes to books, I feel qualified to use a food analogy because I was born and raised in one of the world's great food cities, New Orleans. From the time I was able to eat solid food, I was treated to the spiciness of Cajun dishes; the subtle nuances of Creole cuisine; my mother's rich, maroon spaghetti sauce; and the excesses of home-cooked soul food. When I eat out, I bring that dining heritage with me and apply it to the meal before me. It makes me appreciate great cooking and distinguish it from a meal that's bland and uninventive. Someone who was raised on a basic meat-and-potatoes diet is not likely to experience food the same way I do.

Eating a wide variety of foods heightens all five of our senses. Traveling to new places broadens our understanding of the world and other cultures. In the same way, reading across genres expands a child's perspective and gives him or her mental nodes or connecting points to which he or she can refer in the future.

I recall speaking with an elementary teacher during a school visit about the best readers in her class. The teacher pointed out a young girl who had read all the books in a popular series, and she told me what a voracious reader this student was. I then asked about one of the boys I noticed standing by the magazines, and the teacher explained that he liked to read, but his reading preferences leaned mostly to dirt bikes and sports. I don't know for sure, but I'm willing to bet that boy has comparable reading skills to the girl.

I'm convinced it's important for young readers to read and hear a wide variety of books and stories. You may not be a fan of my book *PEE-YEW!*, which is all about things that smell bad, but I assure you there are children in your read-aloud audience who are fans of books about stinky things. You may not be a fan of children's poetry, but I suspect there's at least one child in your read-aloud group who loves rhyming verse. Please don't misunderstand what I'm advocating. I'm a firm believer fiction has to be a big part of a child's reading (and read-aloud) diet, but it should be only one part of that diet.

> *"Some books are to be tasted, others to be swallowed, and some few to be chewed and digested."*
>
> Francis Bacon

I tell kids to make it a goal to read a variety of books. And they don't even have to read an entire book. I suggest they just choose a book they wouldn't normally pick up and read the first few pages. Maybe they'll want to read more. Maybe they won't. If they don't want to read more of that kind of book, they can keep looking and tasting. Remember, they don't have to chew it and digest it—they just need to taste it!

There is one thing to consider regarding nonfiction/informational books. Because they are based on verifiable facts and are not typically plot driven, informational books do not usually lend themselves to cover-to-cover readings at one sitting. When introducing these books as read-alouds, it's best to share one aspect or subtopic of the book at a time. For example, I wrote and illustrated the book *Backyard Bloodsuckers* (2000). The book contains information about bloodsucking insects, worms, arachnids, and other lovable critters. There's way too much information in the book for a single read-aloud. It would be much more productive and entertaining to choose one bloodsucker (*e.g.,* fleas) and read about them. Choosing one aspect of the book in this way also allows for a much more focused follow-up. One of the wonderful things about nonfiction/informational books is that it's so easy to set-up the reading with activities prior to the read-aloud. In the case of *Backyard Bloodsuckers*, children could make clay models of insects, tell personal stories about bugs, draw pictures of bugs, sing songs about bugs, and so on before ever seeing the book and hearing it read.

Also consider the possibility of pairing a nonfiction book with a fiction book. For example, an informational book about baby ducks would be a nice complement to a reading of the book, *Make Way for Ducklings*.

CHOOSING THE RIGHT BOOK

My friend and acclaimed early childhood educator, Dr. Pam Schiller, has some great tips for picking an appropriate book for your read-aloud:

1. *Read-aloud books should follow the interest of the child. Sometimes children have specific interests and this is an advantage when choosing a book. Other times you will need to think about children in general. Most of them love books about animals, insects, a child their age, and transportation. For very young children, books need to be about things that are familiar to them, such as home, family, cars, and pets. They do not have enough experience yet to understand stories outside of what they already know.*

2. *Books need to hold a child's interest. This means care must be taken to choose a book appropriate in length—one that matches the attention span of a child. As a rule of thumb, toddlers do well with books that are two to three minutes in length. Three- and four-year-olds can handle books that are three to five minutes in length.*

3. *Make sure illustrations are appealing and accurate. Preschool children are very interested in the pictures that accompany the story. Ninety-five percent of preschool children are visually dependent when listening to a story. (See Chapter 14 on page 95 for ideas on books for older children.)*

4. *Books with rhyming words or a repetitive line are a great choice. Children can participate. After a couple of readings, they will soon chime in as you read. Participation goes a long way in maintaining interest.*

5. *Select books with unique vocabulary. Children learn more rare words from books than they do from conversation. This high-level vocabulary will be an invaluable tool when children begin their educational journey through school.*

6. *Make sure to choose some read-aloud books with large print and large pictures. When reading these books, move your finger under the print so children will become familiar with the direction of print and the separation of words.*

7. *Don't over-moralize or over-teach.*

8. *Read from a variety of sources, such as comic strips/comic books, magazines, and newspapers. As long as the content is appropriate, children will enjoy seeing the many places that print is used.*

9. *If children lose interest in a book, put it down, and try again later.*

I want to make a distinction between choosing read-aloud books for groups of children versus choosing books for a single child in a one-on-one situation. In a classroom environment, educators must deal with a variety of personalities, maturity levels, and cultural backgrounds. Not every book will appeal to every child during every reading. You should have ambitious goals for your group read-alouds but realize that even modest progress is still progress. Every read-aloud experience enriches children's lives because an adult has decided that nothing is more important or more urgent than sitting down with a child, opening a book, and reading aloud to him or her.

It's almost impossible to reproduce the intimacy of a one-on-one reading in a group environment. When a child snuggles close with someone who has that child's welfare in mind and reads aloud to him or her, the decision of the adult to forego everything else takes on a greater meaning. When a child gets to choose a read-aloud book that is special to him or her, the child learns that he or she can make choices and that those choices will be respected.

Children need both the cultural enrichment of group readings with one-on-one readings that build intimacy and trust. If you can build a bond with a single child through a read-aloud, you should take the opportunity to do so. But be aware that in the classroom, even group read-alouds convey to children the importance of reading and the possibilities available to them through the written word.

ROCK YOUR QUESTIONS

> *"I am not a speed reader. I am a speed understander."*
>
> Isaac Asimov

Once during a Sunday Mass, one of our parish priests called all the young children up to the altar. His intent was to create an atmosphere similar to a storytelling circle. Unfortunately, this particular priest had spent most of his adult life as a college professor and had little experience dealing with small children.

It soon became obvious the priest had woefully miscalculated the attention span of his young audience. After listening as long as he could, one little boy raised his hand. "Yes," the priest paused and smiled. "You have a question?" "Yeah," the little boy said. "So . . . what's the main thing?" When you read aloud to children, it's going to be important for them to understand "the main thing."

CLOSED-ENDED VERSUS OPEN-ENDED QUESTIONS

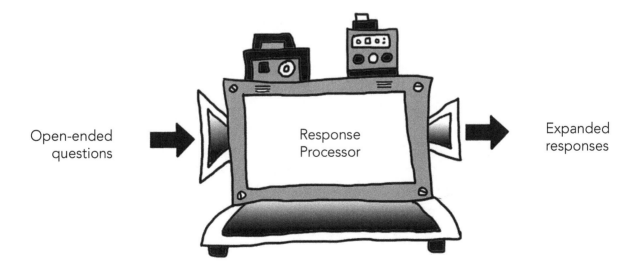

Open-ended
questions

Response
Processor

Expanded
responses

One of the most effective ways to help children understand the main thing is to ask both closed-ended questions (questions requiring only a one- or two-word answer) and open-ended questions (those requiring some elaboration). Here are some examples of both:

Closed-ended questions

- Did you like that story?
- Did the bunny wake up on time?
- Do you think that dog is smart?
- Did that ever happen to you?
- Would you like to have one of those?

Open-ended questions

- What did you like about that story? Not like?
- Who can tell me about a time you woke up late?
- What kind of tricks have you seen dogs do?
- What would you do if that happened to you?
- What are some good things about having one of those?

Questions to Ask Before, During, and After the Reading

Questions before the read-aloud:

- Look at the picture on the cover of this book. What do you notice?
- What do you think this book might be about? Why do you think that?
- Do you know what these words (point to the title) say?
- Do you think that the title might give us an idea of what the book is about?
- These words say, "Written by (author's name)." What does that mean? (Do the same with illustrator if different.)
- Do you think this is a story about real people/animals or imaginary people/animals?
- So, even before we start reading the book, what do we know about it?

Questions during the read-aloud:

- Look at this character (in a picture book). What can you tell me by looking at him/her/it?
- Have you ever felt that way? (after a character expresses an emotion)
- Has that ever happened to you?
- If you were there with the character in this book, what would you say to him/her/it?
- Was what just happened a good thing or a not-so-good thing? Why do you say that?
- How would you fix the problem?
- What else could this character have done?
- How do we know that what he/she/it said is true/right/correct?
- What do you think is going to happen next? Why do you think that?
- Remind me again, what is this character trying to do? What does he/she/it want?
- So, what do we already know?
- Help me remember, what was the problem?
- Tell me again about . . . (refer to earlier event, situation, comment, etc.)
- Wait a minute. Does that make sense? What has changed?
- What do you think is going to happen next?
- Did you think that was going to happen? (after it happens)
- Why or why not?
- Wait. What I just read to you . . . what does that mean?
- Do you think it was right for him/her/it to feel that way? Why or why not?

Questions after the read-aloud:

- If you could ask the main character any question, what would you ask?
- Have we ever read any other stories like this?
- Does this remind you of any other stories we've read? Why?
- How would this story have been different if . . . (insert your own "what if" here)?
- Who did you like best in that story? Why?
- Was there a part of the story that you didn't like? Why?
- Was there some part of the story that you didn't understand?

- If I had not read this book before and I asked you what it was about, what would you tell me?
- Does this story make you think of something that's happened to you?
- What other title could this book have? (This reinforces the "main thing.")
- Did you like the way the story ended or would you rather have seen a different ending? Why?

If you want to pursue a point deeper, continue to ask open-ended questions following each response from the children. Here are some examples:
- How do you know that?
- How did you figure that out?
- Can you tell me a little more about that?
- Can you say that in a different way?

Finally, anticipate the questions your listeners are asking in their own minds but may be afraid or too shy to ask out loud. A child's appreciation and understanding of a story may rest on the answer to one of those questions.

THE POWER OF PREDICTABILITY

Some books lend themselves to audience participation because they have predictable text. Allowing children to verbally provide the predictable text is another way of drawing them into the story. I once wrote a book titled *The Really Weird Pet Store*. It was written in rhyming verse and provided lots of opportunities for students to supply the predictable text. One page of the book shows some very large fantasy animals called Snoods. The text on the page reads:

Or maybe you'd like your own pot-bellied Snood
Who doesn't do much except eat lots of . . .
Can you guess the last word? Of course! It's "food."

A book is a conversation between a writer and a reader. Therefore, by allowing the children to participate by providing the missing word or words, that relationship between writer and reader is enhanced and deepened. Children love to provide the predictable words in a story. Be sure to include a few stories with predictable text when you choose your read-aloud books.

6

ROCK YOUR ENVIRONMENT

When I speak at schools, I'm often in an auditorium, gym, or other large room with a stage. If I'm given the option of being on the stage or on the floor at the same level as my audience, I always choose to be on the same level and as close as possible. I think a close proximity to your audience allows for a more powerful presentation and a more engaged audience. In a classroom or library environment, the room may be smaller, but the idea is the same: The closer you are to your audience, the better. How you actually seat the students depends on the physical dimensions of the room and the personality and characteristics of the group.

SEATING

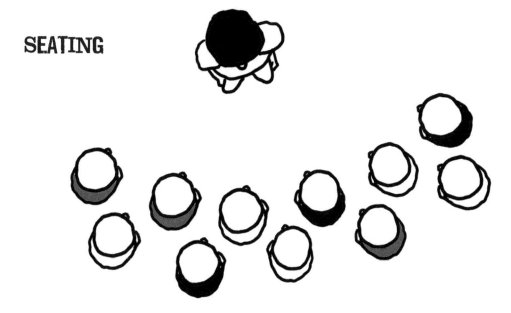

Typically for school read-alouds, kids sit in a semicircle with the teacher (or other reader) at the opening of the semicircle. Kids usually sit in rows or in a random cluster close together. If their behavior allows, I like the random cluster better than rows. It gives the environment more of a group feeling and encourages more interaction and engagement. But you know your students best. Seat them in a way that is likely to achieve the most positive outcome. This might take a bit of experimentation. Once you find a seating arrangement that works, stick with it. Just remember that the younger the child, the more he or she needs the reassurance of a consistent seating arrangement.

For older children, there are alternatives to these seating norms, some of which are wonderfully creative. I've seen reading igloos made from one-gallon plastic milk cartons, tree house reading lofts, and reading pits. One school I visited even had a full-size convertible automobile available for readers in their library media center.

At another school library I visited, the media specialist (with parent help) had built a "campfire" around which she would do read-alouds. The campfire consisted of rolled-up pieces of cardboard crumpled, painted, and formed into logs. These cardboard logs were placed in a circle surrounding some yellow, orange, and red crepe paper which was blown from below by a small fan giving the effect of a campfire. A small red light hidden in the crepe paper added to the effect. The media specialist would lower the lights in the library and then sit crossed-legged on the floor with the children and read aloud. It was amazing!

Think about other places you might read aloud. Perhaps you can sit under a tree on your school grounds or use the playground equipment as a seating area. Children could sit on the slides or swings as you read out loud to them. Or read aloud while the children are crouching under the tables in the library pretending to hide from "wild things."

If you choose to do your read-alouds in a very unusual place, you might want to let your school administration know in advance. Many years ago I illustrated a version of Clement Clarke Moore's *'Twas the Night Before Christmas.* I illustrated the entire book using pieces of torn paper. The publisher took my illustrations and added glow-in-the-dark ink to many of them. When the illustrations were exposed to light and the book was taken into a dark room, the illustrations glowed brightly. It was very cool. A principal I met told me one morning he noticed a teacher walking from her classroom past his office to the janitor's closet with a book and several of her students. She would take the students into the closet and close the door. After a minute or two, the teacher and the students would emerge from the janitor's closet happy and smiling. Needless to say, the principal found this unusual and somewhat disturbing. Turns out the teacher was reading my glow-in-the-dark Christmas book to her students, a few students at a time. The janitor's closet was dark and allowed the kids to get the full effect of the glow-in-the-dark illustrations.

The teacher had the right idea but she could have avoided the uncomfortable situation by putting a medium-size cardboard box on a desk or table and letting students take turns looking down at the glow-in-the-dark book. To create a dark space, the teacher might have draped a cloth over each child's head, creating a one-person reading tent. Cheap, simple, and effective.

A LITERARY LUNCH

One very creative read-aloud idea I've experienced was a literary lunch. The elementary school designated an empty classroom as the "literary lunch" room. During the literary lunch, children brought their food from the cafeteria to the room and a teacher or volunteer read to them as they ate. The children understood not to talk or ask questions. They were there to eat and listen. It was a huge success.

Maybe you don't have an empty classroom in your school, but there's probably someplace where you could have a literary lunch. Maybe a corner of the cafeteria or the gym. Maybe a section of the library. You can limit the size of the audience by restricting the literary lunch to one or two grade levels. The grade levels would also determine what books you choose to read. You can choose whether to finish the book in one lunch period or spread the reading of a single book over an entire week. You know what will work best for your school and your students. But regardless of the venue, the idea of a literary lunch is a winner.

BACKGROUND MUSIC

Consider using background music to help set the mood for your read-aloud. It's better to use instrumental music rather than vocal music because the singer's voice will likely be distracting. Above all, keep your music low-key. Brahms, spa music, or anything similar will probably be fine. If your story involves superheroes, knights, or any scenario where courage is involved, you might choose something

more heroic such as Wagner's "Flight of the Valkyries"—but play it only during the introduction to the story or at the end as a closing.

You can find just about any genre of music you want on one of the online music services like Pandora, or you can do a YouTube search for "spa music" and stream your tunes directly from that site. Of course, you can also bring your own recorded music to your classroom.

LIGHTING

Just a quick note about lighting as part of the environment. It's great fun to lower the lights to create a mood for your read-aloud. This works especially well if the story takes place in a dark forest, an old house at night, a cave, or some similar low-light environment. And if someone flips the light switch off and on rapidly during the reading, it makes for a great "lightning storm" effect. For most children, that's all great fun. But some children are easily and seriously frightened by darkened rooms, and some children with autism spectrum disorders can become upset by quick changes in lighting. Know your audience before you attempt to fiddle with the lighting. And if it's an issue, create the mood in other ways. For example, children could just partially cover their eyes with cupped hands to give a darkened effect to the room.

ROCK YOUR READ-ALOUD READERS

> **"A children's story which is enjoyed only by children is a bad children's story."**
> C.S. Lewis

LINK THE GUEST READER TO THE BOOK

Before most children enter school, their parents or grandparents have read many books to them as a quiet time activity. When they reach school age, these children have teachers or media specialists read books aloud to them. But those are the people the students see every day at school and having them do a read-aloud is very predictable. Granted that predictability works well when the audience is very young. The younger they are, the more they need the stability that comes with seeing the same adult every day. But with older children a guest reader can be an exciting and fun experience.

Here are some ideas to consider for guest readers, depending on the book you're reading aloud:

> **For books highlighting animals, potential readers could be:**
>
> Ranchers, veterinarians, pet store owners or employees, zookeepers, wild animal park employees, animal trainers, specialty animal park (e.g., alligator farms, insect zoos) employees, university entomologists or veterinary school professors, pest control company employees (including companies that capture skunks, squirrels, raccoons from

homes and release them some distance away), kennel employees, staff of your state wildlife and fisheries office, taxidermists, natural history museum staff, nature photographers, beekeepers

For books highlighting weather or the environment, potential readers could be:

Meteorologists from your local TV station or federal weather office, landscape company employees, landscape architects, employees from a local lawn and garden center, plant nursery staff, university botanists, staff from your state or county agricultural extension service, people whose jobs are directly affected by weather (e.g., farmers, airline pilots, fishermen), employees of a recycling center, employees of a local waste disposal company

For books about sports or fitness, potential readers could be:

Local professional, college, or high school coach (active or retired), your school's physical education teacher or coach, sports trainer, local TV sports reporter, sports photographer, owner of a local fitness center or yoga studio, local sporting goods store employee, doctor or sports medicine expert

For books about cars, buses, trucks, trains, boats, planes, tractors, construction equipment, motorcycles, and other vehicles, potential readers could be:

Airline pilots, tugboat captains, taxi drivers, bus drivers, emergency vehicle drivers, firefighters, mechanics, construction equipment operators, TV traffic reporters, motorcycle police, farmers, semitruck drivers, delivery truck drivers, shuttle van drivers, air traffic controllers, anyone who makes a living operating or repairing one of the vehicles in the book

Teachers and media specialists often invite local dignitaries to serve as special celebrity readers. It's common to see news stories or social media posts showing the mayor, a city councilperson, or the school district superintendent reading to a group of students. While we should be grateful these busy people have taken time out of their day to read to our students, it would be difficult to put into words how UNimpressed most students are by public officials. To a young child, politicians and school board officials are just well-dressed adults.

The ultimate celebrities for upper elementary students are your local high school or college sports stars. Having a professional athlete agree to read to students is especially great but not every school has a professional sports team in close proximity. If you can get a well-known local athlete to read to your class, you have struck read-aloud gold. By modeling reading, these athletes can motivate and inspire even your most reluctant readers. Encourage read-alouds by both male and female athletes. That way, all the students have a reading model.

For books featuring people from other countries, invite someone from that country or region to come read the book aloud. Does your reader have a thick accent? Excellent! Kids need to hear other accents.

SENIOR CITIZENS

> **"A man only learns in two ways: One by reading and the other by associating with smarter people."**
> Will Rogers

In 2014, there were about 46.2 million Americans over the age of 65, according to the U.S. Department of Health and Human and Services. They represented 14.5 percent of the U.S. population. People older than 65 are expected to be 21.7 percent of the population by 2040. This age group is a largely untapped resource for your school. While many of these seniors continue to work either full-time or part-time, others have that one important resource many younger adults do not—time. Seniors have time to read aloud to your students and they're just waiting for an invitation.

In order to put the free time of seniors to good use in your school, you actually have to ASK them to come read to your students. Talk to the parents of your students. Ask them to let you know if THEIR parents would like to come and read. Send a note home with your students asking for grandparents to volunteer. Consider calling your local senior citizens center or put up a note on the bulletin board at the center.

SECURITY CONCERNS

Although security requirements have tightened over the years, most school districts have no problem with a visiting reader as long as he or she is accompanied by a teacher or an administrator while in the school building. The biggest issue seems to be whether or not the person reading is receiving payment for his or her time. If you're paying someone to read at your school, most school districts will require the reader to be fingerprinted, notarized, dipped in an anti-bacterial solution, searched, DNA sampled, X-rayed, and approved by the lunch lady. That's only a slight exaggeration. For simplicity's sake, stick to volunteer readers whenever possible.

And be aware there's always the chance someone will be offended by your choice of speakers. Regardless of your personal beliefs, advocacy groups or organizations associated with social activism are risky sources for guest readers. Please do yourself a favor and clear any guests with your school principal beforehand.

STUDENTS AS READ-ALOUD READERS

Among your guest readers, consider recruiting the students themselves. If the time and situation permit, it can be a real boost to a student's confidence to read all or part of a book to the rest of the group. A teacher needs to be aware that he or she may be biased toward picking a popular student or a student who has proven to be a joy to teach. Sometimes the class clown may be the best choice for a guest reader because he has consistently demonstrated serious performance chops. The most important consideration is the student's enthusiasm for the idea of reading aloud to the group. If the student is enthusiastic but struggles with the reading, you can provide some support. Or you might graciously thank the student for his or her effort and complete the reading yourself.

VIRTUAL READERS

Skype, Google Hangouts, and other video conferencing tools make it possible for book authors to do live, online read-alouds of their books to students. Many authors offer free 10- to 20-minute virtual visits while charging a fee for longer visits. Due to an abundance of caution, some school districts block these free video conferencing tools, which is too bad. In those cases, you may want to visit websites featuring prerecorded videos of authors reading their books. Though it's not an interactive, live reading, it is an opportunity for students to see and hear a favorite author. One of the most popular of these websites is Reading Rockets (readingrockets.org). The site has interviews with more than 100 authors, some of whom read from their books.

Need another resource for your virtual read-alouds? If you have YouTube access at your school, type in an author's name along with the word "reading," and you'll likely find one or more videos of that author reading his or her book.

Just as it's best to preview a book before you read it aloud to a group of children, you should preview any videos you plan to show. Usually, videos produced by large publishers on behalf of their authors have been reviewed and screened for content and production values. However, some authors and illustrators produce their own online videos and those safeguards may not be in place.

Some authors and illustrators also monetize their online videos by allowing commercials to be shown on the front end. The content of those commercials can be unpredictable, so you may want to cue up any videos after the commercials and just before the content you intend to share with the children.

A word of warning: As you watch videos of authors reading their books, you may be surprised to learn that being able to write a wonderful read-aloud book does not always mean the writer can deliver a memorable read-aloud performance. Writing and performing are two different skills. The ability to capture and hold a reader's attention requires the writer to engage with the reader. During silent reading, the reader can provide the voice of the writer, but during a read-aloud or a storytelling session, the person doing the reading or speaking provides that voice and, consequently, the engagement.

CARMEN DEEDY ON AUDIENCE ENGAGEMENT

When it comes to telling a story and engaging an audience, no one does it better than master storyteller and TedX speaker, Carmen Deedy. I asked Carmen to share her strategies for engaging her audiences.

Q: If you're not getting the reaction you want from your audience, is there a sure-fire technique you use to get them more engaged?

Carmen: *Even with a strong story, you can still encounter a situation where you are losing your audience. If so, start by paying attention—listening, if you will—to them. Are they laughing in the wrong places? Are they silent? There are two ways out of this situation: Either end the story as quickly as possible, or engage fully with your audience—i.e., make the monologue a dialogue. Ask them questions and let them know you invite their answers. If you get no immediate response, choose a person who looks the most sympathetic and address her or him directly. Rare is the audience that does not respond to this. And use humor, if possible, because no rhetorical device is as disarming as a good laugh among a gathering of strangers.*

Most important, remember the audience is infinitely wiser than we imagine—they know when a story is falling flat, and they know that you know—so speak to them, honestly. And what might simply have been an afternoon or evening of good stories might turn into an extraordinary moment of human connection.

Q: How do you choose which stories to tell?

Carmen: *When I am standing in front of the listeners. The choice is usually made in a split second and is nearly always a subconscious one. I'm not certain I could really tell you what I'm looking for, in totality, but here are a few elements that affect the final decision: What are the demographics of the group? Is this an indoor or outdoor space? What time of day is it? What do I feel like telling today? What kind of mood is the audience exhibiting? All of these elements enter into the final equation. You just hope when you begin that first sentence, and crossed the Rubicon, that you and your subconscious mind have chosen wisely.*

Q: How long does it take you to craft and polish a story to the point you KNOW you've got a winner?

Carmen: *This is always a humbling question. The frankest answer is this: The first half dozen tellings of a new story stink. They do. The next half dozen stink just a tad less, and so forth. If you grit your teeth and continue to hone the story, you might have a little gem of a tale . . . after about 50 tellings.*

Q: How do you keep a story fresh after you've told it hundreds of times?

Carmen: *Everyone has his or her own way around this sticky wicket. My solution is as simple as it is difficult to commit oneself to: I must force myself to be present, present, present. No wandering off, even for a nanosecond; no rote telling; no pretending this audience is like every other audience (because that is a mathematical impossibility). So I push myself, not only to be there with the listeners, but to tell the story as though I were seeing it for the first time—and, if I'm lucky, they will see it too.*

Carmen's comments remind me of a recent conversation I had with a friend. We were discussing how challenging it must be for a musical artist or group to perform the hit songs hundreds or thousands of times before live audiences yet keep the performances fresh. Teachers and media specialists face a similar challenge when they do read-alouds. Educators may have a handful of favorite stories that they read aloud to every grade level, but each year the audience changes. The challenge is to find ways to keep even the most familiar read-aloud story fresh.

Carmen's way of addressing this challenge is to be "present, present, present." And one way to stay present is to move your focus away from yourself and onto the book and your audience. Remember, this is an interactive experience. Watch the children's faces and their body language. Look for aspects of the story you may have overlooked in the past. Try a different voice or venue. Have someone else read the story, and you become an audience member yourself.

The demands of the school day will always make it easier to fall back on doing things that are familiar and predictable. Remind yourself that for most students, much of what they're doing are things they're doing for the first time. Remind yourself to treat each read-aloud story as if it was the first time you're reading it.

READING THE BOOK

The best public speakers in entertainment, politics, sales, professional development, religion, the arts—in fact, in any occupation—are always great storytellers. And the stories they tell are personal stories. Before you even show the cover of the book you're about to read aloud, be sure everyone is seated and paying attention, and then tell a personal story related to the book.

Stories are how ancient people passed along the culture, wisdom, and mores of their group. When someone shares a personal story, he or she takes us beyond our group identity and into the experience of the individual. A personal story reveals some aspect of our unique relationship to the world around us.

We need a common cultural story, but we also seek personal stories about the variety of experiences within that culture.

If I planned to read *The Pout-Pout Fish* by Deborah Diesen to a group of young children, I would begin by telling the children a story about my grandmother. She immigrated to the United States from Sicily and her first language was Italian. In the Sicilian Italian dialect, the word for mushroom sounds a little like "foonjia." That's funny because when you pout and poke out your bottom lip, your lip looks a little like a mushroom. When any of her grandchildren would pout and poke out their bottom lips, my grandmother would say, "Don't make a foonjia!"

After telling that story, I would ask the children to repeat "foonjia" together just because it's fun to say. Finally, I would ask them to show me what THEIR bottom lips look like when they pout. And as soon as everyone was making a pouty face, I would play the role of my grandmother, wagging my index finger and pretending to scold the group—"Don't make a foonjia!" Only after the laughter died down would I hold up the book and begin the read-aloud.

Telling a "story before the story" provides a personal connection and a smooth segue to the read-aloud itself. You can almost always think of some personal story to connect to the book you're about to read aloud. Here are some ideas:

For the book	Tell a story before the story about
The Very Hungry Caterpillar	A caterpillar that ate your tomato plants
Llama Llama Red Pajama	A time when you were afraid of going to bed

Charlotte's Web	Your experience visiting a farm
Brown Bear, Brown Bear, What Do You See?	A visit to a national park when you saw a bear
Miss Nelson Is Missing!	What school was like when you were young

ROCK YOUR PUPPETS

"Raise your hand if you like dinosaurs!"

Dinosaur Dance Party

Consider using puppets to introduce a story or to serve as your read-aloud mascot. Mary Jo Huff is known for her clever use of puppets as part of her read-alouds. I asked Mary Jo to share some of the ways she uses puppets and how they can enhance the quality of a read-aloud. Here's what she had to say:

"Introducing a puppet into a read-aloud adds a visual connection for children. A puppet can present background information, which

will help children make sense of what they are going to see and hear. The puppet can also present the title of the book to be read as well as the author and illustrator information. It can also support the development of thinking skills that help bridge a story and real life.

When it is time to sit down and listen to a story, a puppet can transition children. Using a signal, such as singing a song or repeating a rhyme or chant, makes children aware it is time for a story, and the children will gather.

A mascot can be a valuable tool and an important link for children. Beforehand, the puppet can talk about what you are going to be reading aloud. Thinking questions such as: "Where is he going? What does he need? Are his friends helping him?" will be part of the discussion after the read-aloud. The children can talk with the puppet and answer the questions.

A puppet and puppet friends might be the focus a child needs to get hooked, and the puppet helpers will encourage children to retell the story. They will interact with puppets in a different way, talking with them in full conversation while building their language skills.

I personally do not let the puppet read the story. An introduction, interjection, and conversation before and after the read-aloud works best in my world.

If you have a special puppet like a bear, frog, alligator, rabbit, moose, and so on, you can document the books you will use with a particular puppet and have it available at the read-aloud. Give the puppet a name; and if it is a mascot, it will become part of every child's daily life. A mascot will introduce a new puppet and tell how it is connected to the upcoming story. When the mascot has something to say, the children are always attentive.

There are numerous places to purchase puppets. In addition, printed copies of the characters can be laminated and placed on sticks for the children to use as story props. This is a fast and easy way to extend story retelling. Puppets also can be created with socks, sacks, and envelopes to name just a few items.

Find a puppet that fits your hand and personality, and give it a try with your next read-aloud."

Whether you use puppets depends on your skill and willingness to experiment with them. In some classroom and library situations, the teacher or media specialist may have an aide or a volunteer who enjoys working with puppets and can use the puppet mascot to interact with the kids during the reading. In those cases, the reader does nothing but read the story, and the puppet asks questions of the children during the reading. Example: "Oh no! Kids … do you think he should go into that cave? Is that a good idea?"

Many puppets can serve as passive visual reinforcement for a story. If you have a plush version of the Very Hungry Caterpillar, you don't necessarily have to employ the caterpillar in some animated way during the reading. Simply placing the caterpillar on your lap or on the arm of the chair from which you're reading can build the connection between the plush animal and the story. On a future library visit, children will immediately make the connection when they see the plush animal on the library bookshelf.

DEALING WITH UNFAMILIAR WORDS

"If people say they just love the smell of books, I always want to pull them aside and ask, 'To be clear, do you know how reading works?'"

Bridger Winegar

Once you begin reading aloud, there's a good chance you'll read one or more words that are new to your students. When that happens, show your students the strategies YOU use to figure out the meanings of words, then encourage them to try your technique. Here's an imaginary conversation between me and another person. Watch for the unfamiliar word and notice the sample technique for deciphering its meaning:

Veterinarian: "Mike, when you visit schools and draw with children, do you ever draw animals?

Me: "I sure do, Dr. Vet. And just to keep it fun, I usually anthropomorphize a couple of the animals like they do in TV ads."

Whoa! Hold on a minute. What's that word? "Anthropomorphize?" That's not a word most people use in their day-to-day conversations. Do you know what it means? If you don't, I bet you have a strategy for figuring out what it means. Your strategy may go something like this:

As you look at the word "anthropomorphize," you probably notice words or partial words you already recognize: "anthro" and "morph" being two examples. And you know that words ending in "ize" usually mean that some action is involved. You may even quickly test your vocabulary to see if you know any similar words. Perhaps the word "anthropology" will come to mind. Or if you play videos games or watch cartoons, you already know that when something "morphs," it changes. You might also add the context in which the word is used (i.e., anthropomorphized animals are used in advertising). So you may come to the conclusion that anthropomorphizing has something to do with changing animals or objects into humans when you draw them. And you'd be correct. Anthropomorphizing means giving human characteristics to things that are not human. Like this:

Show your students how you decipher the meaning of unfamiliar words. During your read-alouds, go ahead and read right through a word with which your audience is likely to be unfamiliar, then stop. Ask out loud, "Wait a moment. What was THAT word?" Go back and read the word out loud again as you point to it. Touch each syllable. Ask, "Does anyone know what this word means?" If no one knows the word, offer the strategy you used with "anthropomorphize." Say, "When I don't know what a word means, I look to see if the word is giving me some hints. Do you think this word (point at it again) is giving us hints about what it means?"

Listen for their responses. Acknowledge each one and congratulate the student for his or her input. If any of the students' responses are actually helpful to understanding the meaning of the word, give extra acknowledgment to those responses. If you see a "hidden" word within the word, point it out and ask the children what the "hidden" word means. Model the same strategy you used to figure out what "anthropomorphize" meant.

Context clues are also very helpful. If one character in the book says, "I'm scared!" and another character replies, "I'm not just scared, I'm terrified!" the context gives the reader a healthy hint of the meaning of the word "terrified." By being aware of the context in which the words are spoken, young readers can often approximate the word's meaning.

If time permits and one of your students has deciphered a word, ask him or her how he or she figured it out. You may learn a new technique yourself or at the very least, you'll learn a bit more about that child's reading strategies. And as a bonus, the other kids will hear what strategy a peer uses from the peer himself or herself.

Spend as much time as you think appropriate with the particular technique you choose, then back up and reread that section of the book, taking special care to point to the now-familiar word. Then move on. You may use any strategy that produces results. The important point is to give your students some strategy for digging into words they don't know and discovering what they mean.

In many cases, it will be more practical (given the time limitations in most classrooms) to quickly give the definition of one or more words as you go. For example, in the book *Stellaluna* by Janell Cannon, there's the following sentence:

"Wrapping her wings about her, she clutched a thin branch."

The word "clutch" doesn't readily lend itself to dissection. Here, it would be easier to say, "To 'clutch' means to hold on to something very tightly." If you like, you can ask the students to pretend their index finger is a thin branch. Have them "clutch" their finger with their other hand. Then say, "You are clutching your finger. That's what 'clutch' means." Back up and reread one or two previous sentences to refresh the context, and then continue reading.

The words you choose and how deeply you and the children investigate their meanings will be determined by the time available and your goals for the read-aloud. In general, it's a good idea to limit the number of "word dissections" you make to just three or four at each read-aloud session.

ROCK YOUR VOICE

"Fee, Fi, Fo, Fum . . ."

The easiest way to enhance a read-aloud is to use different voices. Almost everyone does it naturally. For instance, if you're about to read the part of a book where a big, gruff character speaks, you naturally furrow your eyebrows, tuck in your chin, and speak in a deeper voice. If you're reading text during which a tiny animal speaks, you probably raise your voice to a higher pitch. We all understand by varying our vocal delivery, we can help identify the attitudes and roles of the characters in the story. This makes it easier for young audiences to understand who is speaking and whether or not the speaker is happy, sad, mean, or frightened.

Realize that your students are already familiar with your voice. They hear you speak every day and are well aware of how your voice changes when you are happy, impatient, upset, or not feeling well.

When you're reading aloud, you want your listeners to focus more on the voices of the characters in the story than on your voice. Of course, as an introduction to the book or during narrative passages, it is perfectly OK to use your normal speaking voice since you are now part of the story, too. But when the story characters speak, you want the kids to hear the characters' voices.

FOCUS ON VERBS AND ADVERBS

I love nouns. Without them, no one would know what people, places, or things we're talking about. But nouns are not the stars when you're reading aloud. Star status in read-alouds is reserved for the verbs, adjectives, and adverbs. If you know when they're coming in your read-aloud (see Rock Your Preparation on page 20), they can represent an opportunity to provide some wonderful vocal embellishment. For example, here's a sentence from the book *Angelina Ballerina* by Katharine Holabird. Read it aloud in your normal speaking voice with no particular emphasis.

"She skipped over rocks and practiced high leaps over the flower beds until she landed right in old Mrs. Hodgepodge's pansies and got a terrible scolding."

Now, read the sentence aloud again, and this time apply a healthy dose of your own emphasis to the underlined words:

"She skipped over rocks and practiced high leaps over the flower beds until she landed right in old Mrs. Hodgepodge's pansies and got a terrible scolding."

It certainly would have been possible to put the emphasis on other verbs and adjectives and possibly even on the words "rocks" and "pansies" but it wouldn't have sounded as natural. I especially like to play with the word "high" in that sentence. I like to prolong the word and say, "h-i-i-i-gh." It's similar to the way Italians stretch out the greeting, "Buongior-r-r-r-no."

You may find it easy and natural to add vocal variations when reading aloud. But if not, you can build your confidence and skill by practicing putting the emphasis on verbs, adjectives, and adverbs.

Probably the greatest voice-over talent to ever live was Mel Blanc. Mel was a vocal genius who provided more than 400 voices for classic cartoons, many of which you know well. They include Bugs Bunny, Daffy Duck, Tweety Bird, Yosemite Sam, Pepé Le Pew, and Elmer Fudd. Does this mean you have to do 400 voices? Well, yeah—if you can. But if not, there are lots of ways to create variety in your voice. When interviewers would ask him how he was able to come up with so many voices, Blanc's explanation was that he got a lot of inspiration by listening to the voices all around him. If you pay attention, you'll discover there are voices all around you, too. Can you recall a time when you've heard someone with a voice that had one or more of these characteristics?

Whiny

Sing-song

Deep

Timid

Warp speed

Stop and start, distracted

Painfully slow, um . . . uh . . . er . . .

Powerful

Raspy, gravelly

Mumbly

Lisp

Loud

Bossy

Foreign accent

Try this: Pick a few sentences from a book—any book, even this one—and try reading those sentences out loud with a few of the voice types listed. See if it feels a little strange hearing yourself talk like that. If it does, that's OK. All you need is some practice to make you feel more comfortable. Here's something to try:

The next time you're driving in your car, read the billboards, store signs, and street names out loud in one or more of those vocal styles. Note: This is best done when you're in your car alone. NEVER attempt this when you're in the car with your teenage daughter. You're already enough of an embarrassment to her.

REGIONAL ACCENTS

Using a regional accent is a particularly effective way of embellishing your read-aloud. I'm told one of the things that makes my book *Petite Rouge: A Cajun Red Riding Hood* so much fun to read aloud is the fact it's written in a Cajun accent. People from outside southern Louisiana who have never heard a Cajun accent have a blast reading the story in a voice they've never used before. Other readers tell me they love using the Cajun accent because it reminds them of the way their grandfather, cousin, or other relative speaks. And for kids in Cajun country, well cher. Dat's jus' de' way mah Grande Mere she talk.

Think of all the other wonderful regional accents we have in the United States—Brooklyn, Deep South, California Valley Girl or surfer dude, Texas cowboy/cowgirl, Upper Midwestern, to name a few. There are even local variations within those regional accents. I know that's true in New Orleans. There's a distinct difference between the accents of someone who grew up in Uptown New Orleans and someone who grew up in the city's Ninth Ward. If you've ever seen the movie *My Fair Lady* with Audrey Hepburn, you know this accent variety is especially true of the different neighborhoods of London, England. Have some fun with this. Try reciting the alphabet in some of the accents. Or pick an accent and sing "Happy Birthday" or "Twinkle, Twinkle, Little Star" as exaggeratedly as you can. I can almost guarantee you will make yourself laugh out loud.

If you'd like to hear a real accent pro in action, do a YouTube search on "Amy Walker voices." You'll find several videos of Amy doing regional accents, and she includes some tips for trying it yourself. It's fascinating. For even more examples, do an Internet search for "examples of accents and dialects," and you'll find thousands of audio and video links.

SHHH!

Whispered words indicate what someone is saying is private, personal, and not for a general audience. You don't need the author's words to tell you when to whisper. When you come to a place in your read-aloud where you think you should whisper, do so.

In the book, *The Whisper* by Pamela Zagarenski, you'll find ample opportunity to discover how whispered words can seem almost spiritual. And if you've only got a few minutes, try whispering the poem "Fog" by Carl Sandburg. Whispering makes the poem even more powerful.

Just for fun, try whispering a short book you usually read aloud at a normal volume. Set up the reading by telling the kids a grumpy giant is sleeping in the classroom next door or in the hallway and you don't want to wake him up. Don't feel like you need to go into a lot of detail about the giant, why he's there, and so on. Just use it as an excuse to read aloud in a whisper. Treat it like a game. The kids will love it.

VARY YOUR PACING

Pacing is the speed and fluidity of your speech. You can add a twist to your read-alouds by varying the pacing and adding some pauses within a page, a paragraph, or even a sentence. Try this: Read these words aloud at your normal pace. Don't do anything fancy, just read them normally:

"Today is a bright, sunny day and I'm not going to let anyone ruin it, especially Jeffrey Klinglehoffer whose one goal in life is to drive me nuts."

Now, try reading the same sentence again, but this time pause just before you say the phrase, "especially Jeffrey Klinglehoffer." Then pause for a long time after saying the name, as if you're pondering what a miserable human being Jeffrey Klinglehoffer is. Then finish the sentence.

"Today is a bright, sunny day and I'm not going to let anyone ruin it, [pause] especially Jeffrey Klinglehoffer [long pause], whose one goal in life is to drive me nuts."

Do you find the pauses make the sentence more powerful and dramatic? Now, let's add some variety to our pacing and pausing. This time repeat the sentence, keeping the pauses, but read the first part of the sentence a little more quickly than you normally would. And then, when you reach the phrase, "drive me nuts," pause between the words, "drive," "me," and "nuts." Like this:

[Read aloud a bit more quickly] "Today is a bright, sunny day and I'm not going to let anyone ruin it, [pause] especially Jeffrey Klinglehoffer [long pause], whose one goal in life is to drive [pause] me [pause] nuts."

THE POWER OF THE PAUSE

> **"Music is the space between the notes."**
> Claude Debussy

Pauses can make a huge difference in what your audiences hear. Our ears need some quiet time between sounds whether we're talking about music or speaking. Without space between the words in a book or the notes in music, what we would hear would be one long, variable-pitch drone. You may be familiar with that phenomenon. It's much like the sound your child makes when he or she is bored and wants you to entertain him or her.

Stand-up comedians know timing is key to delivering a comic bit. I once took a stand-up comedy course and our final exam consisted of us each performing 10 minutes of original comedy in front of a live audience. It was simultaneously terrifying and exhilarating. As my classmates and I rehearsed in front of each other, I learned the power of pausing and waiting for the joke to sink in. Professional stand-up comedians know an audience sometimes needs a quiet moment to "get" the joke. I recently saw a video of two famous comics talking about the characteristics of great comedians. They agreed a sense of timing (also referred to as "pacing") is crucial. One of the comedians said he believed David Letterman was not the funniest comedian he'd ever seen in terms of his comedic material, but Letterman's timing is so superb that he rates as one of the best stand-up comedians of all time.

Here's your chance to be a stand-up comedian. Say the following joke out loud and use your normal conversational speaking pace. Keep in mind that this joke will likely not be understood by children and may be misinterpreted by them, so it's best to practice telling the joke to another adult or when you're alone in a room or your car.

Two peanuts were walking through a bad neighborhood. One was assaulted ("a-salted").

Funny? Maybe a little. Now try pausing before the punch line:

Two peanuts were walking through a bad neighborhood. [pause] One was assaulted.

It's just funnier if you wait a second before delivering the punch line. In fact, you can wait MUCH longer than you think you should and the joke will work even better.

That's one of the reasons greeting cards work so well to convey a humorous thought. You read the front of the card and then there's a pause as you open it and read the punch line inside. Most greeting cards wouldn't be as funny if all the words were on the outside of the card.

I graduated from college with a degree in Marketing and soon got a job as a salesman. One of the first things I noticed about the really good sales people in my company was that they knew the power of timing. More specifically, they knew when to talk and when to be quiet. The fact is, when we're sitting in close proximity to a stranger (such as in a sales situation with a new prospect), most of us feel a little uncomfortable with lulls in the conversation. Average salespeople tend to fill those lulls with blather. Top salespeople keep quiet and wait for the prospect to say something.

White space is the visual equivalent of silence. Graphic artists know the power of white space and how and when to use it. For the next few days, keep an eye out for the ways advertisers use white space in the print ads you see and in electronic media. The empty spaces on the page or screen give power to the image and, by extension, the message. That's one of the reasons the interiors of art galleries and museums tend to be so stark. In addition to limiting distractions, the starkness makes the artwork seem more powerful.

"It says so much because it says nothing."

In graphic design, white space gives the designer control over where your eye goes. If the screen, wall, page, or canvas is completely blank except for a small red circle, your eyes will naturally focus on the circle. Conversely, if you're looking at an *I Spy* or *Where's Waldo?* book (where there is very little white space), your eyes have to work much harder because there's so much to see. In fact, it's the intent of the illustrator to keep you distracted and to discourage your eyes from focusing on any one item on the page.

There is a Zen saying that it is the space between the bars that holds the tiger. [Personal note: OK, call me shallow, but I still prefer PLENTY of bars (with not much space) between me and a tiger.]

Old gothic cathedrals were built with huge empty spaces, which humbled the worshippers, made them feel small, and represented the presence of God. And it doesn't get more powerful than that.

Teachers know while they're speaking in front of a classroom, it's likely the attention of some children will drift. But when that teacher stops talking and continues to stand in front of the room, children will soon change their focus (for at least a couple of nanoseconds) to see why they can't hear the teacher speaking any longer. In that situation, not speaking is more powerful than speaking. Just as white space can be a powerful focal tool in art, silence can be a way to capture and direct a listener's attention.

FAST FORWARD

> *"I read a book twice as fast as anybody else. First I read the beginning, and then I read the ending, and then I start in the middle and read toward whatever end I like best."*
> Gracie Allen

There may be times when you want to vary your pacing by pressing the fast forward button on what you're reading. To do that, you read a long sentence or group of words very, very quickly, jamming them all together. Master storyteller and author Carmen Deedy is a genius at this. Carmen will begin a story at one speed then suddenly concatenate a string of words together in a breathless vocal sprint. And then—just as quickly—stop, pause, and conclude with a phrase or sentence spoken at an almost glacial pace. Her audience becomes riveted.

This fast forward technique is especially effective when there are phrases or sentences that appear repeatedly throughout the book. We're all familiar with the Christmas song, "The Twelve Days of Christmas." In that song we sing about each of the 12 days, continuing to repeat what the gifts were on all the preceding days. The only breather we get during the song is the phrase, "five golden rings." At some point during the song, many people have an impulse to speed up the lines about the earlier gifts, especially after the line about the five golden rings. It just seems natural (and fun) to do so.

A good opportunity to use accelerated pacing in a read-aloud comes while reading the book *Tikki Tikki Tembo* by Arlene Mosel. This is the story of a young boy who falls into a well and whose rescue is delayed because of the length of his name. There are several variants of Tikki Tikki Tembo's full name, but all versions are long and challenging. Here's a popular version:

Tikki tikki tembo-no sa rembo-chari bari ruchi-pip peri pembo

During the reading, it's necessary to say Tikki Tikki Tembo's entire name many times. Toward the end of the reading, it is fun to hit the verbal "fast forward" and begin saying his name faster and faster. The faster the name is read, the more fun it is to say. Granted, this is an extremely long group of words and the accelerated pacing would work best only after children have heard the book read a number of times at a normal pace. But once they commit the name to memory, they can't wait for the opportunity to join in.

ROCK YOUR SOUND EFFECTS

Adding sound effects to your read-aloud doesn't have to be complicated, expensive, or time-consuming. You can create wonderful sound effects with simple objects you probably already have around your home or classroom. My friend and brilliant teacher, actor, performer, and coach Frank Levy advises educators to look around their classrooms and reframe the objects they see. For example, Frank says to pick up your stapler, invert it, and shake it up and down. Voilà! You've just created the sound of a helicopter. A large diaper bag filled with old pots, pans, and a pizza tray makes a great thunder sound when you drop it on the floor.

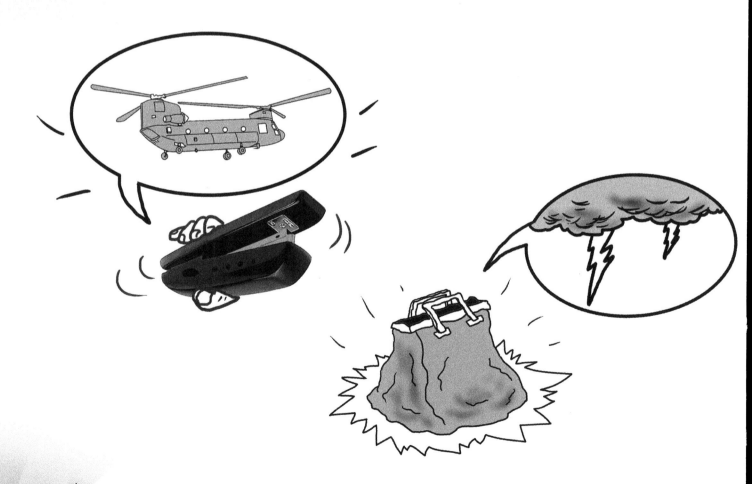

You can find loads of inexpensive whistles, rattles, and other sound-makers online. Frank likes to use Giggletimetoys.com but there are dozens of other sources. Frank uses small slide whistles to reinforce the action of going up or down, and he uses a plastic three-trumpet horn to make the sound of an elephant trumpeting. If you want to go digital, there are several inexpensive, handheld, sound-effect machines. Some have as many as 20 sounds. Just search online for "novelty sound effect toys."

Other ideas:

A cheap keyboard (from a thrift store or yard sale) can make a creepy organ sound if you hold down the key on the far right (highest note) and, while continuing to hold it down, press down the key next to it. Continue holding down successive keys, one at a time, while moving to the left. Five or six notes ought to do it but you can continue moving down the keyboard until you run out of fingers. This is a great classic effect to add tension to a story.

A little sand in a plastic bin or bucket can help introduce a story that takes place in the desert, at the beach, or on an island. Just sift some of the sand between your fingers as you explain the setting for the story.

Leaves in a bin or box can provide a nice visual, tactile, and auditory effect if the story takes place in a forest or during autumn. You can lift some of the leaves and let them gently fall from your fingers. Or crunch them in your hand.

The open end of two large, reusable plastic cups tapped on a hard surface can be horse's hooves.

Have a piece of sandpaper handy and when a character scratches his head or back, scratch the sandpaper.

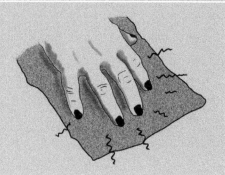

Crinkling cellophane (good excuse to buy and eat a candy bar) sounds like a fire.

Sprinkling rice on a metal baking sheet produces a reasonably effective rain sound. You can also ask around and see if any of your friends or someone at school has one of those "rain sticks" they sell at festivals and gift shops.

Put a hard-sole shoe on your hand and "walk it" on a hard surface to create the sound of footsteps. You can also try putting some dry leaves or coarse sand in a pan and walking the shoe on that.

If your school has a portable sound system that you can use (check with your school's coach or music teacher), put the microphone close to your mouth and add lots of reverb to create the sound of giants speaking (Fee Fi Fo Fum!), animals in caves (bear growling), creaky doors, and so on.

But don't rely on just your own creativity. Tap into your students' natural creativity and ask them to help come up with ways to make sound effects. Ask them, "Does anyone have an idea how we could make the sound of a chipmunk popping out of the ground?" Or "We need to make the sound of a fish swimming. How could we do that?" Once they're personally invested in the telling of the story, they'll be much more engaged and the book will become more memorable. The trick, Frank says, is to make your stories multidimensional. You can add dimension by involving the students in adding sounds and actions.

Frank says he gives students a cue. For example, he will have the students make the sound of a strong wind blowing when they hear him say the word, "wind." Frank lets them practice a time or two to ensure the group's blowing sounds are of an appropriate length and volume. For background crowd noises, students can use a popular technique used by directors for years. Just have the kids say the word "rhubarb" over and over. It sounds just like a group of people mumbling.

Years ago, I remember watching comedian Victor Borge on TV. Borge was a brilliant classically trained Danish pianist who was a regular performer on TV, especially when variety shows were popular. In spite of his classical training, Borge was a class clown at heart. In one of his comedy bits, he would sit at a grand piano, place some sheet music on the music stand, and then he would begin playing beautifully. Very quickly, he'd reach a point in the music where he hit an obvious wrong note. He stopped playing, smiled sheepishly at the audience, and began again. He would continue to make the same mistake at the same spot until eventually he would stop and take a very close look at the sheet music. Then Borge would lift his hand and flick an imaginary fly off the sheet music page. The next time he played the piece flawlessly. The audience realized Borge had seemingly mistaken the fly on the sheet music for one of the notes and that's what was causing the problem. That sudden realization by the audience plus Borge's hilarious irreverence for something considered "serious" made for great laughs.

As part of his act, Borge had a clever technique to audibly represent punctuation marks. He would read a passage from a book aloud and wherever there was a punctuation mark, Borge would make a silly sound. Search YouTube to see a video of Victor Borge using this "visual punctuation" technique he developed.

I've adapted my own set of sounds for punctuation marks that I think work well with today's kids. Here's a list:

When you see this punctuation mark	Make this sound
Question mark	Huh?
Period	Car brakes screeching
Dash	Woosh
Exclamation point	Woosh then car brakes screeching
Comma	Woop
Quotation marks	Kissy sounds

Those are just the sounds I like to use. You can apply whatever sounds you would like. Or you can ask your students to create their own sounds. When you or the kids get a chance to apply this technique to what's being read, no one's attention drifts because everyone is anticipating making the next silly sound. This technique also subtly drives home the awareness that different punctuation marks have their own unique roles to play in the written word.

CHAPTER
11

ROCK YOUR PROPS AND COSTUMES

L et's assume you have this many good ideas for read-alouds:

and this much money to work with:

You can still rock your read-aloud props. The shelves of post-holiday decorations at your local dollar store are a great source for props. The day after July 4, Christmas, Easter, Thanksgiving, Halloween, and other holidays, you can pick up flags, masks, headbands, noisemakers, and other crazy props for pennies on the dollar.

Can't wait for the holidays to buy your props? Need a specific kind of prop now? Here's your answer: 4 x 8 feet (1.2 x 2.4 meter) sheets of rigid foam insulation board. Foam insulation board is possibly the greatest material ever invented for making cheap, safe props. Go to your local building materials store and buy a sheet of this stuff. You'll find it with the other insulation products. Foam insulation boards are lightweight, firm, and easy to cut with a box cutter. You can paint it, glue paper to it, and cover it in a mixture of white glue and water to increase its sturdiness.

Here are a few props you can make with it:

Shield

Sun and cloud

A map of your state

Need a talking mirror, a TV/computer screen, a close-up of the narrator's face? Cut an 18 x 24 inch (46 x 60 centimeters) piece of foam insulation board and then cut a rectangle out of the middle of that piece of foam. All you need is the foam insulation board, a box cutter, and some duct tape or clear packing tape (buy the strong stuff). And possibly some adhesive bandages if you're a klutz.

You may use the foam to make a stationary background prop, such as a tree or a mountain, that will help set the scene, but you may also want to create props that have some movement. For example, if you take a piece of foam insulation board and cut a rectangle door from it, and then use tape to create door "hinges," you will be able to open and close the door for emphasis as you read aloud.

If the prop you're using becomes an active part of the read-aloud, and you are reading a picture book, you'll probably want to have an assistant move the prop as you flip the pages of the book, or you may want to move the prop yourself and have your assistant turn the pages of the book.

You might wonder why you would want to use an active prop when you're reading a picture book aloud. Doesn't it seem as though this would distract from the pictures in the book? Not necessarily— especially when you want to add some animation to your read-aloud. For example, if a character in the story is moving from one place to another, you can first have your audience look at the picture of the character in the book and then have an assistant move a foam cutout of the character from one place to another. It might be from one side of the reading rug to the other, or if the sun is rising or setting in the story, your assistant can move the sun prop accordingly.

Want other prop ideas? Frank Levy likes to pull a bolt of blue cloth around and between a group of seated children to simulate a river. And Frank says an empty washing machine/refrigerator shipping box (free if you ask at most appliance stores) is one of the most versatile props you can have in your repertoire. A refrigerator box with windows and a door can be a castle, a rocket ship, Dorothy's house from *The Wizard of Oz*, a cabin in the woods, a storefront, a drive-up window, or any one of a hundred other places. Washing machine/dryer boxes can be smaller houses/rooms or giant rocks behind which kids can hide. If you're silly enough, you can read the book from a window inside the refrigerator box. Just cut arm holes so you can hold the book. Remember, a box has six sides, so you have at least that many options for using it as a prop.

Creating a prop does not have to be a major art project, which is good news if you're artistically challenged. You can create a small prop by making a photocopy of an image from the book; gluing it to a piece of insulation board, poster board, or cardboard; and cutting the backing material to fit. Is this a copyright violation? Probably not.

You're not reproducing artwork from the book for resale or in order to avoid purchasing another copy of the book. You're using the artwork to reinforce the story. Most publishers have no problem with you copying a few images or a limited amount of text from one of their books for classroom use, and they often say so on the title page of many books. If you're really concerned about copyright infringement, you can create a generic prop that is similar but not an exact copy of any image in the book and serves the same basic function.

If you don't consider yourself handy when it comes to creating props, you probably know someone who is. It's likely you have a friend, relative, coworker, or theater arts major who would love to help you create some props. In fact, this is a wonderful opportunity for you to get your school's art teacher involved in your read-alouds and tie in literacy with art. For example, arrange with your school's art teacher to do "fish prints" after reading *The Rainbow Fish* or any other fish story.

If your school has a theme for the year, you may be able to tie that in as well. One year my wife's school had a classic movies theme. I made a giant box of popcorn for the entrance to her library. It was made out of —you guessed it—foam insulation board and some of that goopy expanding foam insulation stuff in a can. It was a huge hit. Here's a picture:

Here are some other foam insulation board prop ideas: Cut some notches into one of the long sides of a piece of foam insulation board and paint it gray. Add a few dark gray rectangles, and you will have a functional castle wall behind which you can read a book about knights, princesses, or dragons.

Cut the board into a long knife-blade shape. Cut triangles for fins. Cut windows. Paint it to look like a rocket ship.

Cut a simple school bus shape. Add windows. Paint it yellow.

Cut a simple tugboat or sailboat shape. Cut some waves and glue them on. Paint the waves blue. Paint the uncut board blue. Paint an ocean/lake/underwater scene. Paint a diver on it and cut an opening in the diving helmet for your face. Paint a diving helmet diver rather than a scuba diver to avoid issues surrounding swimsuits and body shapes.

The options are endless. Flip through some of the read-aloud books in your classroom, see if you notice any typical backgrounds or locations, and reproduce some of those on your foam insulation board.

ENLIST THE GUYS

Does your school have a Dads' Club? If so, there are probably several guys in that group who have some woodworking skills. If you want props that are more permanent, ask the Dads' Club members to build you some simple scenery out of wood. Quarter-inch-thick paneling is very inexpensive and, like foam insulation board, can be cut into just about any shape. And since it's wood, anything you make with it will be more solid and will be able to stand up better to the inevitable bumping and moving around. If you don't have a formal Dads' Club, then ask for help at your next PTO/PTA meeting. Worst case, send a note home with your students asking parents with woodworking skills to contact you.

"We need volunteers to help build the reading loft in the library. . ."

"And now the awards for perfect attendance . . ."

Don't discount the previous paragraph. Like senior citizens, dads are a huge pool of largely untapped talent. A lot of them will jump at the chance to build something for you. And if some of the dads work in construction, they'll often be able to provide the materials from their company at no cost to you. Please note that I'm using the word "dads" here instead of "dads and moms" because I'm too lazy to type the extra words. If you have moms who are skilled woodworkers, then by all means enlist their help as well.

Believe me when I say you must actually ask dads to build what you need for your classroom or library. If you're waiting for them to offer to help build something for you, you'll be waiting a long time. This is based in the well-documented genetic flaw of most of us men, which renders us unable to observe the obvious. If you want a guy's help, you're going to have to actually ask him for help. If you're not sure what I'm talking about here, my wife will be happy to provide examples from our marriage. I acknowledge that some men have evolved to the point where they are able to anticipate your classroom needs. If a man seizes on opportunities to volunteer or build things for your classroom, I tip my hat to him and congratulate you on your good fortune.

KIDS AS PROPS

There's one other source of props you've been overlooking: the students themselves. Frank Levy tells how he creates the whale from *Pinocchio* by having groups of students stand up, face each other, lean forward, and arch their hands above their heads until their fingers touch. This creates a tunnel effect. Each subsequent pair of students crouches lower and lower as they taper the "whale" until they reach the "whale's tail." At that point, Frank has a student lie on the floor with his or her feet touching at the heels. On cue, the student wiggles his or her feet to create the "whale's tail."

For the story of *Aladdin*, Frank asks the students if anyone can do a cartwheel. That student becomes the large door in front of the cave, and when Aladdin says, "Open, Sesame!" the student cartwheels from in front of the cave allowing Aladdin to enter.

If the story requires a table, a student on all fours instantly converts to a table. A student standing straight with his or her arms

held out in odd positions can be a tree. This doesn't always involve theatrical talent. Any student can be a rock or a stump. Enlist your students' help and get creative!

The more you use props as part of your read-aloud, the more you'll be moving into the area of storytelling rather than story reading. In those cases, the book becomes more of a script for the story rather than the sole focus of the children's attention. The degree to which you use props will depend on your goals and preferences.

ROCK YOUR COSTUMES

> *"I have lots of costumes. You never know when you're going to have to dress up like a milkmaid from the 1600s."*
>
> Zooey Deschanel

Elaborate costumes are usually not practical for read-alouds because they have to be made, they take time to put on, and they have to be stored afterward. Again, time is the limiting factor here. But there is one easy costume essential Frank Levy recommends—hats. By donning a baseball cap and pretending to chew gum, a reader can add a delightful performance element to a reading of "Casey at the Bat."

Pirate hats, cowboy hats, berets, three-cornered Revolutionary Era hats, pith helmets, pioneer sun bonnets, and other easily-acquired hats add so much to the reading of a story without requiring special care and handling. You can find them at yard sales, thrift stores, and by asking friends and relatives to donate any old hats they might have. And if you wait until after Halloween, you can get great deals on dollar-store costumes.

One other simple costume idea: those little plastic animal noses with the elastic that stretches around your head. There's a wonderful variety of them, they're inexpensive, and they're easy to put on and take off. A read-aloud of *The Duckling Gets a Cookie!?* by Mo Willems is even funnier if the reader is wearing a plastic duck bill.

ROCK YOUR GESTURES AND BODY LANGUAGE

Gestures and body language can dramatically enhance your read-alouds. Early in my writing and illustrating career, I had the good fortune to spend time at a number of literacy conferences with legendary children's author Bill Martin. At one conference, Bill and I slipped in the back of the room to watch Steven Kellogg recite his story *The Island of the Skog*. All Steven had was a large tablet of paper on an easel and a large black marker, but he made his reading of the story exciting, dramatic, and high-energy. The marker flew across the tablet as Steven created simple images from the book as he told the story. And when it came time to turn a page, Steven would sometimes tug s-l-o-w-l-y on the edge of the sheet of tablet paper and coax the page away from the binding, one perforation at a time. When the action in the story heated up, Steven would violently RIP the page from the tablet's cardboard backing. We were all mesmerized, and at one point, Bill Martin leaned over to me and said, "Isn't it wonderful how Steven can make the simple tearing of a piece of paper so dramatic?"

For some people, gestures come naturally. For others, it's an acquired skill. If you fall into the latter group, here are some things to practice as you learn to incorporate gestures into your read-alouds:

When you're reading about	Do this gesture
Something up high	Lift your hand and point toward the sky. Look up.
An injury, hurting	Touch your body where the injury occurred.
Listening, hearing	Cup your hand by your ear. Cock your head.
Thoughts, thinking	Stroke your chin, look up.
Shouting, calling	Cup your hand on the side of your mouth.
Something shocking, scary	Cover your mouth with your hand, bite your nails, squeeze your eyes shut, shift your eyes from side to side.
Bored, sad	Hold your face in your hand.
A sudden catastrophe	Gently slap the top of your head. (Oh no!)
Ordering someone to stop	Put your hand straight out, palm forward.
Being quiet, a secret, hiding	Point index finger up, place it over your mouth (Shh . . .).
Being brave, strong, courageous	Put one (or two, if possible) hands on your hip/s. Stick your chest out.
Trying to sneak up	Look slowly to the left, then right. Lift your shoulders.

ROCK YOUR RECORDINGS

If you've ever dreamed of hosting your own TV show, recording your read-alouds is a great first step. Recording your read-alouds can serve several purposes. First, children can watch the video in whole or in part at the end of the school day when it's too late to start a new activity. Secondly, the video will come in handy during allergy season when your voice sounds like that of a Division 1 college football coach after a loss. And thirdly, there's something oddly magical to a child about seeing his or her teacher or media specialist on a big screen.

Many schools begin their day with video morning announcements. Typically, two or three students serve as the on-camera talent and deliver the school news, weather, and cafeteria menu. Other students work behind the scenes running the cameras and sound. If your school does video morning announcements, you probably have access to a mini-studio with all the A/V equipment you need to record and edit you reading books aloud. You can do these recordings with or without an audience, and you can invite your volunteer adult readers to come in at a mutually convenient time to do their recordings.

If you're not lucky enough to have a video studio at your school, you may want to rely on the item of technological wizardry that has changed our lives: the smartphone. If you have a smartphone, you have all the basic recording equipment you need to record a read-aloud. Of course, you need to get permission from the parents if your recording is going to include the faces of children, but one way around that is to position yourself so that you and the children are facing each other and the person doing the recording faces you so that you can only see the kids from the back. In fact, you don't really need to include much video of the children at all. Just begin the recording with a wide shot facing you, and show the children from behind to establish that there is a live audience. Then have the camera/smartphone operator zoom in and fill the screen with you and the book you're reading as you do the introduction. Once the intro is over, have the camera operator zoom in on the page of the book you're reading.

Alina Celeste is an internationally touring musician who has recorded some wonderfully delightful YouTube read-alouds. I encourage you to take a look. Here, she offers her thoughts about read-alouds and some great tips for creating read-aloud recordings.

"As with any performance, the first and most important rule is that you should love the material. Love is infectious, so when you present a new story, book, or song with the enthusiasm and joy that accompanies love, you are already hooking the kids. Now that I have a regular following, I also ask my viewers, 'What books do you love? What do you think I would love?' Always begin with love.

Once you choose a book, start thinking about how you might present it. I have a big, silly, loud personality. That works well for story times, but it isn't the only way. Your own style when interacting with children can be applied to your readings. Do you speak quietly and tend to notice small details? Do that when exploring the pictures in the book. Do you ask lots of questions and enjoy conversing with kids? Ask questions while you read. One of the best parts about a live reading is that the book is only part of the whole experience; you and your audience make up the other part. An effective story time is dependent upon all three parts coming together in a unique, singular experience.

How to prepare a book for a live reading:

Step one: Read the book to yourself. Think about different ways you could approach it: What about the story do you find particularly interesting or funny? What do you wish there was more of? What can you highlight in the illustrations that might go overlooked otherwise?

Step two: Read it with a child. Ideally, I'll read a book three or four times with a child, or even a small group; having their input and gauging their reactions is invaluable. They'll often notice things you didn't, ask questions that never occurred to you, or laugh in unexpected places. I try not to carry any expectations into an early reading so as not to affect the child's experience.

Step three: Record yourself! Watching yourself, especially in the beginning, can be tough, but it is also really useful when training yourself to work in front of an audience. Don't worry as much about your mannerisms; instead, concentrate on your volume, your posture, how you hold the book, and how often you look out at your audience. This can be done easily and cheaply with any smartphone.

A note about step three: In the beginning, I found the hardest part about recording was the lack of an audience. I have been a live performer for many years and the camera simply doesn't compare to a roomful of kids! If at all possible, have someone in the room with you and read to them. It doesn't have to be a child, just a person. Human interaction is key to a warm experience."

We've all had the experience of hearing a recording of our voice and being surprised by the way we sound. We ask, "That's not how I really sound, is it?" The answer is, "Yes. That is how you sound."

Teachers and media specialists often record my presentations at schools and conferences and e-mail me video clips. When I view the clips, I'm always surprised to find that I'm not as animated as I assumed. During my presentations, I sometimes get the feeling that I'm over the top with my gestures. When I see the video clips, I realize that I'm certainly moving around and gesturing, but I'm not doing anything that approaches hyperactivity.

The wonderful thing about recording yourself is that the recording device is completely objective. A friend may or may not give you an honest review of your performance, but a recording device will always tell the truth. Watch and listen to yourself reading. Imagine you're a young child hearing you read the story for the first time. Make note of the ways you could improve the reading and then record yourself a second time. You will almost certainly do a better job on the subsequent reading. It may be hard to critique your performance, but you'll be much happier with the results.

CHAPTER 14

READ-ALOUD TIPS FOR PARENTS

Although this book is written primarily for teachers and media specialists, I'd like to address parents specifically. A parent should be a child's first and most important reader. There is no substitute for the time a child spends hearing his or her parent read aloud. This is strange territory for some parents, either because they themselves were not read aloud to by their parents and have no model for that activity or because they lack the confidence in their ability to read aloud well.

Dr. Michael Shoulders has written wonderful books, some of which are appropriate for quiet read-alouds and others that encourage high-energy rapping. Here's some advice Michael has for parents who are unsure about their read-aloud skills:

"I'm often invited to Family Literacy Nights at schools. I spend the first 20 minutes reading to the children. To be honest, I'm modeling

to the parents how much fun reading aloud can be. The second part of the night I talk to parents without their children present. 'Reading aloud to your child is the number one way to create a reader,' is how I begin my talk.

Many parents push back and tell me they don't feel they can do as good of a job as I did. They feel incompetent. I give parents the following suggestions to help make books come alive.

1) Pick the right book.

The greatest factor in a business' value is 'location, location, location.' We've heard it a thousand times. The same can be said about a book. The greatest factor for a read-aloud's value is 'selection, selection, selection.' Not all great books are great read-alouds. To make a book come alive, it has to be a book the reader loves. A perfect example is Bark, George *by Jules Feiffer. I love this book with its variety of animal sounds. I have read* Bark, George *hundreds of times. Each time I share it, it feels like it's brand new.*

2) Don't be afraid to laugh at yourself.

Reading aloud should be a fun time for a child. If the book is silly, the reader's job is to get the listener to laugh. Take it as a challenge. In Bark, George, *when the veterinarian reaches 'deep, deep, deep . . .' (there are 11 'deeps' in a row on this page), I read each word slower and in a deeper voice. I try to strain my voice to get it as deep as I possibly can. Do not fall into the trap of feeling every character in a book needs a different or weird sounding voice. They don't. LISTEN to the story. It will tell you when a voice or sound is needed.*

3) Become an actor.

When I read My Little Sister Ate One Hare *by Bill Grossman, I ACT totally disgusted when the sister eats two snakes or eight worms. If children don't react with a chorus of EWWWWs, I've failed."*

Many parents understand the importance of reading aloud to very young children, but reading aloud can also be a powerful experience for older children. As the reading material becomes more challenging, parents can address a child's reading reluctance by introducing him or her to short stories. A quick Internet search will provide links to thousands of stories that are appropriate for older children. Look for classics by O. Henry or Edgar Allan Poe. Naturally, before reading the story aloud to a child, an adult should determine if it is appropriate for their young reader.

Another option for older readers is poetry. Don't assume a reluctant reader will hate poetry. Try reading *The Crossover* by Kwame Alexander about two brothers who are junior high basketball stars. It's a novel written in verse. It's powerful, it's relevant, and it lends itself to an enthusiastic read-aloud.

Another option is to read a few excerpts from a novel. By choosing exciting or interesting excerpts from different novels, parents can give their children an idea of the variety of reading material that is available to them.

The novels you choose to read from will be determined by the child's areas of interest and reading level. A good place to start is with classic novels like *Gulliver's Travels* or *Alice's Adventures in Wonderland.*

The media specialist at your child's school or the children's librarian at your local public library can help you select books that will stretch your child's reading muscles. Ask those professionals for their suggestions, and be sure to choose a mix of classic novels as well as more recent books.

Dr. Pam Schiller offers even more advice on book choice for older elementary schoolchildren:

"Allow elementary children to choose their own books. It ensures their interest, and it also teaches them to become skilled at selecting books on their own. Start by asking the child about his or her interests, and then pick a few simple books (not too easy and not too difficult) from which he or she can choose.

Select books with interesting vocabulary. Children learn three times more high-level vocabulary from books than they do from conversation. Introduce the unusual vocabulary before reading the book or before the child reads the book on his or her own.

Take a trip to the library to demonstrate the wide variety of reading material available: fiction, nonfiction, reference, research periodicals, and news.

When children enjoy a book by a specific author, look for more titles by this author.

When children choose a book that is beyond their ability, solve this by reading the book together.

Children learn to read one book at a time. Keep plenty of books around at home and at school."

SUMMARY

Time is the new currency. We will happily trade our money for opportunities to save time. We hire people to clean our houses, mow our yards, prepare our meals, and serve those meals to us without requiring us to leave our vehicles. Some even give our kids a toy with every meal! We find it much easier to write a check to a charity than to appear in person and offer to help and we cannot stand to wait in traffic or in an airport line because we feel as though we're wasting time. The vast majority of us can't even go to the bathroom without using our phones while we're there. Talk about multitasking!

When I speak to groups of educators, I tell them everyone in their personal and professional lives wants only one thing from them. And that one thing is MORE. More attention, more effort, more results, more reports, more documentation, and more passion. I recall being a salesperson many years ago, and if I had a good year and met my annual sales quota, I was rewarded by having the size of my sales territory reduced and my sales quota increased for the following year. If you're a teacher, you understand this concept. I visit many school districts every year, and I have never been in a district where the administration said, "You know what? I think these kids have learned just about enough." To the contrary, the push in most districts is for more of everything. And typically, teachers are somehow expected to deal with these ever-increasing demands by miraculously working it into their day.

Is that going to change? Not likely. And that means your time will continue to become ever more valuable. That's why enrollment in time management seminars is booming, and it's why every motivational speaker on Earth has a surefire, multistep strategy for reducing your stress and making you twice as productive. We're all trying to find as many ways as we can to save time as if those little bits of time can somehow be stored in a plastic baggy.

So if your time is precious and you choose to spend it reading aloud to a single child or a group of children, what message are you sending to that child or those children? You're telling them what you're doing is something important and special. You're demonstrating by your investment of time that reading a book together and stopping to let them ask questions and exchange thoughts is an experience of great value. You're demonstrating that reading is one of the things we do with people we care about.

HOW you read aloud is almost as important as WHAT you read aloud. The way you read a book aloud sends a message to your young listener about your attitude toward the subject matter, the characters in the book, and even the act of reading itself. Reading aloud is not a passive activity. To be done well, it requires you to have a goal, a focus, and a level of enthusiasm that conveys the importance and fun of what you're doing.

As with social customs, mores, and traditions, children learn when we model good reading for them. They need to see the adults in their lives reading and enjoying it; and they need to share what they've learned and appreciated about books they've read with their peers.

Remember that reading is a form of communication. The word "communicate" comes from the Latin, "communicare," which means "to share or to make common." When we read, we share the author's experiences, imaginings, or discoveries. When we read aloud, we also share all that with the child with whom we're reading. And most amazingly, when we read aloud we also have the privilege of bringing ourselves TO the book.

Be sure to demonstrate by the WAY you read aloud to your young readers that they can learn to bring themselves to the books they read as well. You can do it. You have the skills. Now go out there and rock your read-alouds!

APPENDIX

TABLE OF CONTENTS

REFERENCES

Interview citations

Brod Bagert
http://www.brodbagert.com/
Alina Celeste
http://www.alinaceleste.com/
Carmen Deedy
https://carmenagradeedy.com/
Mary Jo Huff
https://storytellin.com/
Frank Levy
http://www.storiesinmotion.com/
Pam Schiller
http://pamschiller.com/
Mike Shoulders
http://www.michaelshoulders.com/ms/Site/Welcome.html

Quotations cited in the text

Page 8: Hesse, Hermann. 2009. *Siddhartha*. Random House Publishing Group. Pg. 121

Page 11: Quindlen, A. 2010. *How Reading Changed My Life*. Random House Publishing. "intro section"

Page 15: Dahl, R. 2013. *The Missing Golden Ticket and Other Splendiferous Secrets*. Penguin.

Page 20: Canfield. From an interview with *The Economic Times* a division of *The Times of India*, published Feb. 10, 2010: http://economictimes.indiatimes.com/magazines/corporate-dossier/chicken-soup-for-the-souls-jack-canfield-and-his-mantra-for-success/articleshow/11825464.cms

Page 24: Krieger, R. 2007. *Civilization's Quotations*. Algora Publishing. Pg. 138

Page 28: Bacon, F., & Spiers, A. 1851. *The Essays or Counsels Civil and Moral by Francis Bacon*. Whittaker & Company. Pg. 171

Page 31: Asimov, Isaac. 1995. *Yours, Isaac Asimov: A Lifetime of Letters* Doubleday. Pg. 141

Page 40: Lewis, C.S. 2002. *Of Other Worlds*. Houghton Mifflin Harcourt. Pg. 24

Page 44: Will Rogers Memorial Museum & Birthplace Ranch
http://www.willrogers.com/quotes

Page 54: Winegar, https://twitter.com/bridger_w/
status/610659313711869952

Page 65: Green, B., & Gallwey, W. T. 1986. *The Inner Game of Music*. Ancho Press/Doubleday. Pg. 55

Page 70: Allen, Adler, B. 2001. *Funny Ladies: The Best Humor from America's Funniest Women*. Andrews McMeel Publishing. Pg. 51

Page 87: Deschanel. "Girls in the Woods" *PaperMag*
http://www.papermag.com/girl-in-the-woods-1425148060.html?ad=728x90

BOOKS CITED IN THE TEXT

Artell, Mike. 2000. *Backyard Bloodsuckers*. Tucson, Arizona: Good Year Books.

Ages: 9 and up
Grade levels: 4 and up

Artell, Mike. 2001. *Petite Rouge: A Cajun Red Riding Hood*. New York: Dial Books for Young Readers.

Ages: 5–10 years
Grade levels: K–3

Cannon, Janell. 1993. *Stellaluna*. Boston: Houghton Mifflin Harcourt.

Ages: 4–8 years
Grade levels: PreK–3

Holabird, Katharine. 1983. *Angelina Ballerina*. New York: C.N. Potter.

Ages: 3–5 years
Grade levels: PreK–K

Kellogg, Steven. 1993. *The Island of the Skog*. New York: Puffin Books.

Ages: 5–8 years
Grade levels: K–3

McCloskey, Robert. 1988. *Make Way for Ducklings*. New York: Puffin Books.

Ages: 3–7 years
Grade levels: PreK–2

Mosel, Arlene. 1989. *Tikki Tikki Tembo*. New York: H. Holt and Co.

Ages: 4–8 years
Grade levels: PreK–3

Novack, B.J. 2014. *The Book with No Pictures*. New York: Dial Books.

Ages: 5–8 years
Grade levels: K–3

Pfister, Marcus. 1992. *The Rainbow Fish*. New York: NorthSouth Books.

Ages: 3–10 years
Grade levels: PreK–5

Rasinski, T.V. 2010. *The Fluent Reader: Oral & Silent Reading Strategies for Building Fluency, Word Recognition & Comprehension.* New York: Scholastic.

Thayer, Ernest. 1989. *Casey at the Bat*. New York: Platt & Munk.

Trelease, Jim. 2013. *The Read-aloud Handbook*. New York: Penguin Books.

Young, Ed. 1989. *Lon Po Po: A Red-Riding Hood Story from China.* New York: Philomel Books.

Ages: 4–8 years
Grade levels: PreK–3

STATISTICS CITED IN THE TEXT

Page 44: U.S. Department of Health and Human Services: Administration for Community Living
https://aoa.acl.gov/Aging_Statistics/index.aspx

POPULAR READ-ALOUD BOOKS

If you do an Internet search on "best read-aloud books," you'll get millions of hits. Rather than visit all of those websites, you may want to rely on the suggestions and reviews from booksellers' websites and the websites of some of the educational and literacy organizations listed on page 110. The following is a list of some popular books that lend themselves to read-alouds. The age levels are approximations, so you should review each book prior to reading it aloud to determine if it is appropriate for your audience.

Many of the books listed below have been published recently, but be sure to reach deep into your library for older books that can still capture a child's attention. Many books by Dr. Seuss and Bill Martin work as well with children today as they did with their parents a generation ago.

Adler, David A. 2016. *Don't Throw It to Mo!* New York: Penguin Young Readers.
Ages: 6–7 years

Andreae, Giles, and Guy Parker-Rees. 2012. *Giraffes Can't Dance.* New York: Cartwheel Books.
Ages: 4 and up

Arnold, Tedd. 1987. *No Jumping on the Bed!* New York: Dial Books for Young Readers.
Ages: 4–6 years

Artell, Mike. 2001. *Petite Rouge: A Cajun Red Riding Hood.* New York: Dial Books for Young Readers.
Ages: 5–10 years

Bean, Jonathan. 2013. *Building Our House.* New York: Farrar Straus and Giroux.
Ages: 3–6 years

Beaty, Andrea. 2016. *Ada Twist, Scientist.* New York: Abrams Books for Young Readers.
Ages: 5–7 years

Boudreau, Hélène. 2013. *I Dare You Not to Yawn.* Somerville, Mass.: Candlewick Press.
Ages: 4–8 years

Brown, Peter. 2010. *Children Make Terrible Pets*. New York: Little, Brown.
Ages: 4–7 years

Bunting, Eve. 2006. *One Green Apple*. New York: Clarion Books.
Ages: 4–7 years

Bush, Laura, and Jenna Bush Hager. 2016. *Our Great Big Backyard*. New York: Harper.
Ages: 4–8 years

Byrne, Richard. 2014. *This Book Just Ate My Dog!* New York: Henry Holt and Co.
Ages: 3–6 years

Cronin, Doreen. 2007. *Bounce*. New York: Antheneum Books for Young Readers.
Ages: 1–8 years

Dahl, Roald. 1988. *Matilda*. New York: Viking Kestrel.
Ages: 8–12 years

Dale, Jay. 2017. *Lea's Reading Adventure*. North Mankato, Minn.: Capstone.
Ages: 4–7 years

Dale, Jay. 2017. *Min Monkey and Little Lemur*. North Mankato, Minn.: Capstone.
Ages: 4–7 years

Davis, Kathryn Gibbs. 2014. *Mr. Ferris and His Wheel*. New York: Houghton Mifflin Harcourt Publishing Company.
Ages: 6–10 years

Daywalt, Drew. 2013. *The Day the Crayons Quit*. New York: Philomel Books.
Ages: 3–7 years

Deedy, Carmen Agra. 2014. *Cows for America*. Atlanta, Georgia: Peachtree Publishers.
Ages: 4–8 years

de la Peña, Matt. 2015. *Last Stop on Market Street*. New York: G.P. Putnam's Sons.
Ages: 3–5 years

Gassman, Julie. 2016. *Do Not Bring Your Dragon to the Library*. North Mankato, Minn.: Capstone.
Ages: 3–7 years

Gravett, Emily. 2006. *Wolves*. New York: Simon & Schuster Books for Young Readers.
Ages: 4–8 years

Henkes, Kevin. 2015. *Waiting*. New York: Greenwillow Books.
Ages: 4–8 years

Higgins, Ryan T. 2015. *Mother Bruce*. New York: Disney–Hyperion.
Ages: 5–8 years

Hucke, Johannes. 2009. *Pip in the Grand Hotel*. New York: NorthSouth Books.
Ages: 4 and up

Judge, Lita. 2016. *Hoot and Peep*. New York: Dial Books for Young Readers.
Ages: 3–5 years

Klassen, Jon. 2011. *I Want My Hat Back*. Somerville, Mass.: Candlewick Press.
Ages: 4–8 years

Koehler, Lana Wayne, and Gloria G. Adams. 2016. *Ah-Choo!* New York: Sterling Children's Books.
Ages: 4–8 years

McCarty, Peter. 2015. *First Snow*. New York: Balzer+Bray.
Ages: 4–8 years

O'Malley, Kevin. 2005. *Once Upon a Cool Motorcycle Dude*. New York: Walker & Company.
Ages: 6–10 years

Polacco, Patrica. 1998. *Thank You, Mr. Falker*. New York: Philomel Books.
Ages: 5–8 years

Prelutsky, Jack. 1996. *A Pizza the Size of the Sun*. New York: Greenwillow Books.
Ages: 6–10 years

Rathmann, Peggy. 1995. *Officer Buckle and Gloria*. New York: Putnam's.
Ages: 4–8 years

Reagan, Jean. 2014. *How to Babysit a Grandma*. New York: Alfred A. Knopf.
Ages: 5–8 years

Rex, Adam, and Christian Robinson. 2016. *School's First Day of School.* New York: Roaring Book Press.
Ages: 4–8 years

Rinker, Sherri Duskey, and Tom Lichtenheld. 2011. *Goodnight, Goodnight Construction Site.* San Francisco: Chronicle Books.
Ages: 1–6 years

Rocco, John. 2013. *Super Hair-O and the Barber of Doom.* New York: Disney–Hyperion Books.
Ages: 4–9 years

Rosenstock, Barb. 2014. *The Noisy Paint Box: The Colors and Sounds of Kandinsky's Abstract Art.* New York: Alfred A. Knopf.
Ages: 4–8 years

Rubin, Adam. 2012. *Dragons Love Tacos.* New York: Dial Books for Young Readers.
Ages: 3–7 years

Rueda, Claudia. 2016. *Bunny Slopes.* San Francisco: Chronicle Books.
Ages: 3–6 years

Russell-Brown, Katheryn. *Little Melba and Her Big Trombone.* New York: Lee & Low Books.
Ages: 6–10 years

Rylant, Cynthia. 2005. *The Stars Will Still Shine.* New York: HarperCollins.
Ages: 4–8 years

Shannon, David. 1998. *A Bad Case of Stripes.* New York: Blue Sky Press.
Ages: 4–8 years

Stein, David Ezra. 2010. *Interrupting Chicken.* Somerville, Mass.: Candlewick Press.
Ages: 4–8 years

Willems, Mo. 2013. *That Is Not a Good Idea!* New York: Balzer+Bray.
Ages: 4–8 years

Willems, Mo. 2016. *The Thank You Book.* New York: Hyperion Books for Children.
Ages: 4–8 years

Yolen, Jane. 1987. *Owl Moon.* New York: Philomel Books.
Ages: 3–7 years

READ-ALOUD WEBSITES

The best place to begin your search for read-aloud book videos is YouTube. If you don't have a particular book, author, or subject in mind, just do a YouTube search on "read-aloud books for children," and you'll get more than 100,000 results. If your search phrase is something more specific, such as the title of a popular book or the name of a popular author, you are likely to find thousands of additional links. If you prefer links with more information about the age-appropriateness of a book or ways to extend the book to various curriculum areas, you'll have better luck with one of the links below. As always, you should review the video prior to showing it to children to ensure that it is appropriate for the age level. It's also a good idea to cue the video past any advertisements.

http://www.justbooksreadaloud.com/

This site states, "This site is JUST books read aloud by normal (but enthusiastic) readers." Books are organized by length (short, medium, long) and by language.

http://www.storylineonline.net/

This site is produced by the Screen Actors Guild American Federation of Television and Radio Artists (SAG-AFTRA). The site features celebrities reading one of several dozen books. Reading times range from about five minutes to a little more than 16 minutes.

http://www.barnesandnoble.com/

If you visit the Barnes & Noble site and click on a children's book, you may find a link to a video of someone (sometimes the author) reading the book aloud. Not all books have videos, so it's hit or miss.

http://www.indypl.org/readytoread/?p=6150

The Indianapolis Public Library provides links to YouTube videos of 100 books being read aloud, often by the author him/herself. This site has some overlap with the www.storylineonline.net site, but it's well worth visiting. There are also some live readings with children. Fun!

http://pbskids.org/lions/stories/

Between The Lions is part of the PBS Kids site. The site contains story videos overlaid with text. The site has so many things going on that it can be a little distracting, but the videos are built around solid educational content that's fun. It's worth a look.

http://www.getcaughtreading.org/

This website is maintained by the Association of American Publishers. It sponsors National Readathon Day, and the website has free posters (or a small fee for up to 12 posters) showing sports and entertainment celebrities reading. The site also has a list of activities to support the message of the posters.

ORGANIZATIONS PROMOTING READING AND LITERACY

http://www.rif.org/
http://www.literacyworldwide.org/ (ILA)
http://read.gov/kids/
http://www.reachoutandread.org/
http://www.ncte.org/
http://www.buildon.org/
http://www.826national.org/
http://www.familieslearning.org/
https://www.firstbook.org/
http://www.barbarabush.org/
http://www.bookadventure.com/Home.aspx
https://www.bookshare.org/cms
http://www.read.gov/cfb/
http://www.cbcbooks.org/
http://www.imaginationlibrary.com/
http://www.familyreading.org
http://www.freereading.net/
http://www.guysread.com/

Maupin House
capstone

At Maupin House by Capstone Professional, we continue to look for
professional development resources that support grades K–8 classroom
teachers in areas such as these:

Literacy	Language Arts
Content-Area Literacy	Research-Based Practices
Assessment	Inquiry
Technology	Differentiation
Standards-Based Instruction	School Safety
Classroom Management	School Community

If you have an idea for a professional development resource,
visit our Become an Author website at:

**http://www.capstonepub.com/classroom/professional-development/
become-an-author/**

There are two ways to submit questions and proposals:

1. You may send them electronically to:
   proposals@capstonepd.com
2. You may send them via postal mail. Please be sure to include a
   self-addressed stamped envelope for us to return materials.

Acquisitions Editor
Capstone Professional
2 N. LaSalle, 14th Floor
Chicago, IL 60602